# THE MAN CONFUSED BY GOD

Bennet Mermel
and Rosalie Cushman

In memory of my brother, Kalvin Mermelstein, whose life I saved
and my best friend, Moishe W. Weis, whose life I could not.
*—Bennet Mermel*


To Carol Scott whose help on the manuscript has been invaluable
and, as always, to Sam Sabzehzar, whose love is boundless.
*—Rosalie Cushman*

Nothing happens
until something moves.

—*Albert Einstein*

# CHAPTER 1

"A woman, she's Hungarian, makes this cake for me. It is wonderful." He draws out the word, emphasizing his affection.

After a beat, he says, "but you can't have any." Bennet is all playful energy, popping up and down at the far side of the table, making his way to the counter where the cake sits.

"Oh?" I question in that soft-sided way, knowing my excess weight is in evidence. Is he teasing me?

"You need to gain weight and I need to lose it," I offer tentatively.

He slices me a piece anyway. It is a miracle it holds itself together, it is so incredibly thin—a mere sliver, a torte of some kind, with coconut and a bit of cream between the cake layers. He licks his fingers after placing this cake shred on my plate and hands it back before cutting an only slightly larger piece for himself.

I am struck by the itty bitty piece he has cut for himself, which seems odd to me if he loves it so much.

"You need a bigger piece to gain weight. Eat more food," I bully. It may be a game we are starting, still testing the limits of a tentative friendship. I decide to take my chances with the small bit of advice that I define as directive but my own family would describe as bossy. I am guessing he may know a thing or two about bossy so I'm willing to be a risk-taker here.

Today, prior to the cake, each of us has had one small piece of chicken, a bit of fish from a jar, and half an avocado. The man eats like a bird, and I'm wondering if this is a habit left over from being in the concentration camps. Or, it may be his dedication to preserving his health, limiting fat intake, pacing his overall consumption along with the discipline of walking two and a half miles each day. Even thin, he seems to be the right size, although I can tell from pictures that he does not carry as much meat on his bones as in earlier years. Still, his skin seems clear and reasonably taut, age-spotted some but not much. And while his hair is gray, mine has his beat in grayness, hands down, even though I'm thirty years younger. Bennet carries his body with a younger man's velocity, purposeful and sure, claiming every ounce of life he can, and proudly so.

Without his knowledge, I have already sniffed out the delicate but stalwart aspects of a generous man, frugal in his own life maybe, but capable of giving so much of what he has to others. After all, he has not needed to feed me, yet it seems such a natural thing for him to do, much like breathing. Regardless of what he has in the cupboard, his impulse is to share, like an arm reaching out transferring energy from one source to another. It may be that he hides some of his generosity in other areas from too many prying eyes, but I may or may not ever be able to confirm that hunch. I'll have to wait and see.

For now I'm quite focused on the cake—along with my main purpose for being here, which is to explore Bennet's memories and create a credible history of his experiences during multiple stays in concentration camps and several death marches during World War II. But not only that. As usual, I will want much more. While his traumatic and unusual experiences pivoted him in a new direction, it is my intention to identify and reveal much of the rest of the man as well. The literal events are remarkable enough but I have already come to know that this is no ordinary man sitting in front of me.

No, turning Bennet into something cohesive and solid, putting flesh onto bone, unlike the skeletons we've all seen pictures of at Auschwitz or Buchenwald, will be no small task for I've discovered he reveals himself quite generously at will but has also honed the skill of self-editing to a fine art. He's a hider, this one, not much different than the rest of us maybe, but he has some compelling reasons we don't all share. Yet, I am to find out only later what a lovely set of contradictions old Bennet is, delicately balancing the joy of revelation against no small amount of darkness that invaded his life during the Nazi era.

But first things first. For now I have set my sights on this microscopic piece of cake. "This is fabulous," I tell him.

"Mmmmm," he erupts in the simplest, most primitive of sounds. "It is so good," he responds with a sort of happy growl. He takes serious pleasure; it comes from some place deep, the kind of place that is primitive and personal, but also quite universal. I recognize it in myself but don't feel comfortable enough in his presence yet to make the same sound even though everything in me feels just as primitively moved by this small confection. He is right; it is quite delicious, delectable even.

Like an industrious elf, he has cleaned our plates off the table and, after lovingly wrapping the remainder of the cake, he has sneaked quickly to where there is another cake hidden from sight. He brings me back a different kind, also torte-like but without coconut this time.

Is this possible? My piece is even smaller than the first one. At this point I have abandoned looking at the size of his piece—too upsetting. "I like the first one best," I say. "This one is okay, but the coconut one is better," I offer. Food has an emotional meaning for most people. I know it is complicated for me. But I suspect it has an even more intense meaning for Bennet, a meaning beyond the obvious 'staying alive' function that was so fragile in the camps. I speculate that food brings Bennet both pleasure and comfort, although my hunch is that the deprivation of it from the camp days ratchets the intensity of each emotion. He seems to alternate his respect for food as fuel, basic and elemental, with primitive delicious worship, with the kitchen table serving as altar for both emotions.

How did this man survive the camps he was in, not to mention all the death marching he did, on bread, water, thin soup, with an occasional potato, I wonder. To me it is a miracle he sits before me; the kind of miracle that is meant-to-be, although I have come to know quickly that Bennet is highly suspicious of miracles, even though he most likely is one. Why, just the other day when we were talking he told me "I wasn't supposed to survive."

"Yes you were," I stated with firmness.

"No, I wasn't," he told me with a bit of irritation in his voice.

"Yes, you were," I press.

"No, I wasn't," he nearly hisses, as he slaps the arm of the couch, his eyes penetrating.

At that moment I looked up to catch a small but determined bit of energy blasting out of his clear-eyed face, enough to let me know I should back off just a bit and let him have his way on this belief of his. Perhaps he survived in part because he is just this willful. Later on I come to know the near reverence he carries for his own fortitude—a reverence I will come to share as our time together unfolds.

However, at that moment he had set me straight. Did I smell a small whiff of survivors' guilt—a potent force in nearly anyone that sees death up close and lives to remember it? The memory of watching lives fade away from your vision—some quickly, some quite slowly—is one that repeats itself, an image hard to eradicate from one's mental view of the world.

But I have moved ahead of Bennet's story.

Bennet clears off the table, with me handing my plate back to him. "Thank you for lunch," I say.

"I may not always have food when you come, you know." This of course makes me laugh on the inside because I suspect this man has enough money to buy an entire grocery store. But what do I know?

"I can bring lunch next time," I offer.

"I will always have yogurt and cottage cheese," he says, and I am suspicious our lunches may turn out to be about way more than food anyway.

■

# CHAPTER 2

Bennet tells me things in blunt, short sentences, and writes pretty much the same way—a literal describer if there ever was one. He provides the skeleton, waiting for the listener to fill in the rest. He reveals what he wants to, but keeps far more to himself, I suspect. He may have come by this naturally, partly a result of being orphaned early in life as well as the tight lips required in the camps later on. I noticed his straight manner of speaking and thinking when I read his account of his life given to me by his daughter, Laura. I met Bennet on paper first. Intrigue quickly followed, which ultimately set us on a trajectory to share his story with others. Today's conversation will allow me to begin to put into context the man I first came to know from his written recollections.

I was born in a little village called Zdenevo, in the Carpathian Mountains just south of the Polish border. Our village was part of the Carpathian State, part of Czechoslovakia. When the Hungarians occupied the region, it took on the name of Szarvashaza (land of the deer). During World War II, the Russians occupied the area and named it Zdeniovo. And after Perestroika, the partition of Mother Russia, the same state was taken over by the Ukrainians. If I were to visit my hometown today, I would need a Ukrainian visa.

Already I am interrupting. I learn Bennet was born Benci Mermelstein. I try to imagine him in another place, mountainous and cold, instead of this southern California palm-tree landscape. It is hard. What sits before me is a slightly tanned, remarkably robust eighty-seven-year-old

Bennet, the caretaker of desert turtles, not fearing wild animals. While he is short in height, his feet are solidly planted on the ground, and he displays a life force that is large. To sit in a room with the man is to know its force. You have to share the oxygen with him, he's just that commanding.

Undoubtedly, part of what is to come is his Old World European quality, too, a renaissance energy that undoubtedly has served him well—an unlikely combination of his education and self-learning, a physical ruggedness, yet a perceptible fragility that he apparently tries to hide. As I look around his living room, I see evidence of a traveled creature, artifacts from all over the globe, unique, tasteful, interesting items. They are reflective of not just a traveled man but a curious one at that. They make me curious myself—about him. What is going on in his skull, I wonder. Picturing him coming from a small hamlet tucked away in another era seems like a fairy tale, a story made up to entertain me, although I swear a fairy tale I'd not only like to believe in but to be in if only briefly—at least until the horror begins.

And so I will indulge myself in his Carpathian saga as he leads me back to Zdenevo.

The village had a population of about three hundred and fifty families, the majority of whom were Ukrainian. The other inhabitants were of German, Hungarian, Czech, or Jewish origin. Altogether, there were twenty-three Jewish families.

Oh dear, I must stop myself again. In my mind Jewish is a religion, not a nationality. Bennet has named nationalities, not religions, except for his own. I am to learn at least some of the power of this fusion of identities, of a tribe of people more potent than borders, more profound than blood. And even given the fact that identity is arbitrary, it certainly carries a person (at least initially) through so much of a life, shaping how the world is viewed and what life rafts one clings to. This is no less true of Bennet, incubated in Zdenevo, nurtured through the early years of his childhood, and shocked during the concentration camps, with Jewish vapor trails following behind him all of his life.

To be Jewish from that era is to carry your cultural heritage on your back, however heavy the load. Jewish identity is not considered lightly, not done without serious intent and awareness. In Bennet's case, there seems to be a reverence, a religiosity even, about it, having a sense of community that is profound. Not like America today. Not even like Israel today. No. He is another experience of being a Jew altogether, at least from where I sit.

> A little river ran from the northern to the southern edge of the town, and in the summertime we would swim in it. My father would often take me to the river with him, where he would cleanse himself instead of going to the ritual bath. Our home did not have electricity—the only structure that did was the factory. We had large petrol lamps, and no running water.
>
> However, we had our own well, which contained the best water in the village. You had to lower a wooden pail attached to a wheel to hoist the water up and out. If you were less than four feet tall, you could not do this. Usually our household staff brought the water into the house. Because we had no running water, we had an outdoor toilet near a stall. In the winter it was not very comfortable or pleasant to walk outside to use it. At night, the young children would urinate in a pot indoors.
>
> The village had just one main street, with three side streets. Our house was located in the middle of this main street. Our address was number nine. We had a five-room house with a big porch that could convert into a Sukkah on the harvest holiday when the roof had to be exposed to the sky. We would open the roof of the porch, and during the eight days of the holiday, we would eat there.

Being a marginally trained gentile, I, of course, do not remember much from the Old Testament. I learn from Bennet that the Sukkah symbolizes the tents the Jews lived in when they left Egypt. They were to spend forty years in the desert before they were able to get to the Promised Land. These traditions bind the Jewish sense of community in ways unfamiliar to me. For Bennet, they seem like hinges holding windows and doors to both past actions and future promises. Of course this community is to be fractured from itself during World War II. I know I have to steel myself. Not because I don't know the general history of Jewish annihilation. I do. I've just never seen it sit across the room from me.

■

# CHAPTER 3

I phone Bennet to check on the name of the town he was born in. "Was it Zdenevo both before and after the Hungarians took it over? Or the Russians? And how do you spell it? Is it Zdenevo or Zdenievo?"

"The Ukrainians spell it with an 'i'. The name is the same except for that," he corrects. "It's in what I wrote down," he tells me.

"Yes, yes, it's the vowel I was concerned with. You know vowels?"

Silence. Have I irritated him?

I change the subject.

"Have you eaten lunch yet?"

"Yes, enough; I had mushroom soup. My daughter gets it from Henry's Market. Like my mother used to make. It is delicious." I hear that happy growl again, the pleasure of it all dripping from his voice like soup from a spoon. But now I am fixated on his reaction to more than this simple bowl of soup. I am also hearing the memory of his mother, the comfort it brings him, and the taste of his Carpathian life, threading its way through him, sturdy and sure. I think back to the personal account of his life.

Father and Mother slept in separate beds, and all of us children shared beds. Sometimes at night I would wake up afraid. When I was three or four years old, I remember going to Mother's bed, softly begging her to let me stay with her. She often heard me and took me in, even though we were not allowed to wake a parent. However, sometimes if father heard me, he would take me in, too, and that was a big treat. Their beds were nice and soft, with feather pillows and covers.

My parents operated a general store, attached to our living room. It was a long, wide structure, with a warehouse that had large bins for different kinds of grain, and a basement where perishable items were kept. The store had no refrigeration but relied on blocks of ice that were cut from the river in the wintertime, and kept in a dark building over the summer. My friend Nate's father owned the building; he was also the beer distributor for all the villages around.

Our kitchen was a big room. It had a wood-burning stove and another wood-burning oven, and two large credenzas—one for meat dishes and one for dairy. This was required if our house was to be kosher. We strictly observed the rules about kashrut. If by accident one of us used the incorrect dish, we had to sterilize it, and if we mixed up the knives, we had to stick them in the ground for a few days. There was also a big table in the middle of the kitchen. At night this table was converted into a bed where the servant would sleep. Next to the kitchen was a service porch, with a big steel kettle in which we boiled the laundry.

"What do you think of that?" Bennet asks after we have gone over a good portion of his account over the phone.

"Tell me about your food. What were meals like then?"

I try to envision all the work involved in keeping kosher in the 1920s with no running water or electricity. But maybe it was easier without processed food to worry and wonder about.

"For breakfast we'd have cooked cereal, oats or corn, usually with hot milk. Sometimes eggs, sometimes rice with milk," he tells me. His voice almost quivers when he describes it. I can tell he's got a great and glorious picture in his mind's eye. It comes alive for him and for me as well.

"Lunches we would have a big meal, things like soup—my mother made the best soup. We'd have stuffed cabbages, pasta with cheese or poppy seeds, onions sometimes, and potatoes. Pancakes and latkes with beets or prunes," he adds. "After school but before Cheder mother would give us bread—a kind of flat bread—with butter and scallions sometimes, or garlic from the garden.

"Mother baked on Tuesdays and Fridays. She was the best cook, the best baker. Everyone loved her cooking and baking. She taught all my sisters and they became the best, too. Mother would make cheese Danish, kugel, bread, kokos, among other things.

"Dinner was usually lighter. We would have things like herring, potatoes, maybe rice with cinnamon," he adds. "Overall, we had a rich kitchen. Friday night was a big dinner, too, and Saturday lunches were big," he ladles out to me, with obvious pleasure.

The aliveness in Bennet's voice—it is stunning. I try to picture a smaller version of him with brown hair and smooth skin. I imagine him to be scurrying around a table, trying to sneak a latke while no one is looking, maybe even a cheese blintz, chewing it fast so no one can tell. I hear great affection and fondness for this past as he is describing it. I wonder: after the literal experience of being fed by a mother he apparently adored, could Bennet, in some secret subconscious corner, have fed himself with just such a scene during the camps' starvation years? Perhaps the calories of earlier meals remained in his body and soul. Yes, I think it may have helped. How powerful the memory serves us not just with sad pictures, but more importantly with happy ones, a different kind of sustenance altogether, fueling one forward.

"The squirrel is in my kitchen looking for peanuts, snooping," he says abruptly. "She's jumped up on the sink and can't figure out how to get out." He giggles. You'd think Bennet had just witnessed a moon-landing, he's so excited.

"What…..Right now?" I ask.

"Yes, I leave my kitchen door open and she just comes in. The male won't come in but the female does," he adds. "When I've been gone and she sees me come back, hears my car, in about two minutes she shows up, looking for peanuts. She takes one to her den. Then, in a little while comes back for more.

"Can you imagine?" He echoes through the phone.

His excitement moves up, the pitch rising. I see the Disney-like scene he has drawn for me, wishing I were there in person, right this very second. Not just to see the squirrel but to see him watching the squirrel, taking in the utter delight of it all.

We end our conversation with me returning to what he has written. I feel myself to have entered into another world altogether.

My father, Eisig Mermelstein, was born in 1878 in Pavlovo, about 18 kilometers from Zdenevo. He had two brothers and two sisters. His father's name was David, and his mother's was Esther. He had come to Zdenevo to teach and to help in the general store owned by my mother's father. My mother's father, Leibish Teichman, was married to my grandmother Chana. They had six children—three boys named Kalman, Yidl, and Shoil, and three girls name Reisel, Malka, and Bella. My mother was Reisel, born in 1889.

My grandfather traveled to Poland to buy merchandise for the general store. On one of these trips he contracted typhus, a usually fatal disease, and after just a short while he passed away. My father was in his twenties then. The family and friends suggested that he marry the widow, who was in her early thirties. However, my father did not like this idea—and neither did his family in Pavlovo. He decided instead to marry the oldest daughter—Reisel, my mother—who at that time was all but sixteen years old.

Shortly after their marriage, my mother gave birth to their first son Leibish, after just seven months of pregnancy. Father used to tell us that Leibish was the size of a teaspoon, and they would wrap the baby in cotton. The young couple loved children, and a new one was born every two years until we numbered ten.

I cannot imagine this. No running water, no electricity. It must have been very difficult. A world from the past yet part of it resides in my present. Oh, Bennet, how did your mother do it, I wonder?

We were a large, happy family, all of us delivered by the same midwife, Maria, and numbered as follows:

Leibish (later called Aryeh, born in 1906);

Shary (1908);

David (1911);

Esty (1914);

Bella (1916);

Hudji (1918);

Cilly (1920);

Benci (myself, 1922);

Kalman (later called Kalvin, 1925);

Shimi (later known as Steve, 1927).

It occurs to me that this is a lot of people to be ripped from, to keep track of when you are to be in numerous labor and concentration camps, some serving as transits, not to mention on death marches. I turn my head away from this list. These children have faces. And I don't want to look just yet.

# CHAPTER 4

My father ran my grandfather's store. After some years a fire burned down the house and a new house was built to take its place. I was aware that my father was a very intelligent, self-taught person. He was brilliant in mathematics, and spoke perfect classical German, Hungarian, Ukrainian, Yiddish, English, and the language of the Gypsies, which he had picked up in the army. He learned English because an American family had wanted to adopt him. Earlier in his life, he had accompanied the family to Venice, but kept his promise to his mother and returned to Pavlovo.

He also played the violin. On Saturday evenings he'd play with a young man named Shlomo Stern. I loved to listen to them. If I awoke and heard them playing, I would feel touched by the music and cry. Often the whole family would sing along with them, especially during the cold winter evenings.

And so it seems that Bennet comes by learning—and music—naturally. The two facilities may be equal parts environment and genetics. Clearly, they serve as a context of communication greater even than the content of what he sings or says. They are the carriers of Bennet, a delivery system of sorts, of the content of his character. I see this seed was planted and fostered by his father early on.

"Every Saturday afternoon my father would lay down with a book," he tells me in the here-and-now from the couch where he sits today. So Bennet witnessed the idea of knowledge, incorporating it into his psyche with the deepest of imprints, just like ducks. It will not be without its tensions, however, as soon it will take on a more serious tone; a compulsory learning experience is yet to occur, one over which he will have no conscious choice.

"If I wasn't a perpetual student, where would I be?" He speaks firmly.

This is a point I will not resist for clearly I have my own attraction to learning that is deep and profound. After all, if that were not the case, why would I even be in Bennet's house, in his life, right now? 'Education, education, education' is to become a battering ram, a mantra piercing through his life and his unborn children's, serving a scattershot prompting action, always.

What is it about ideas, learning, knowledge that humans are drawn to? Moths to flames it seems. Learning is intoxicating and sobering; lovely and alarming, all.

And music? It may be the escape from the world of form at just the right moments in one's life. At times when I listen to music that moves me, it seems to rearrange some interior quality of me. Music operates from its own energy system, yet penetrates through us in ways we intuitively know, even if we are unable to describe it for others. I see this in Bennet, this movement.

Zdenevo boasted a large lumber industry, and the lumber mill was the main employer in the village and its vicinity. The head of the lumber company took a liking to my father, and got him involved in the business. Eventually my father became a partner in the mill, which took on the name Gruenberger and Mermelstein. They brought the lumber from the forests nearby by horses. Workers at the mill would cut the wood into different sizes. In the winter, the horses pulled sleds loaded on the front with wood. In the summer, wagons were partitioned, carrying different sizes of wood.

Inside the mill, six big cutters would bob up and down. Sawdust was taken in wagons to the river; a big pile of sawdust burnt there at all times. We kids would actually take our baths at the factory. We'd ask Dad to give a note for the attendant, ordering him to fill the pool with warm water, where we would play and bathe. (We also would beg Dad to write little notes to Leibish if we wanted chocolate from the store, for children were not allowed to enter the store whenever they wanted to.)

The factory also produced pine shingles. Horses took the finished lumber to Mukachevo or Svalyava. Years later, the company that owned most of the forest built a track to cover the long distance from Zbyny to Svalyava. From then on, a small train on narrow rails took all the lumber to Svalyava. While my father operated the lumber mill, my mother ran the store and raised the children. Even though she had some help running the household, she still did all the cooking and baking. When my brother, Leibish, reached adolescence, he helped in the store, as did my sister, Shary. Slowly my father accumulated land and constructed a building that he rented to the government to house the Gendarme, the border police.

We were happy and well. Maria also took care of my mother when she had headaches. We would run to her to beg Maria to come to our house. She would take a sheet to cover Mother, and would burn flax in a small bowl over the sheet. This was a home remedy at that time, one thought to relax and remove the pain. When we were little, we would watch how the flames would dissipate. Afterwards, Mother would fall asleep, waking up to find that often the headache was gone.

Bennet later tells me of a superstitious practice his mother undertook if the kids were sick, to ward off the "evil eye" from a man in the village she felt had a bad aura.

"She would take a cup of water and ten coals from the stove, then mix a soot mixture and put it on the kids' faces to 'cure them'—to protect them," he tells me.

The picture of this for me seems almost mythic—exotic, sometimes superstitious maybe, but peaceful. Even with what would be presumed an understandable difficulty in conducting ordinary daily life, Bennet describes his early childhood environment as comfortable and easy, often serene. Even in describing illness or hardship, he rarely claims a negative perspective. In fact, it seems quite the opposite. Much of his early life is a happy place, coming out of him like happy notes raised from one octave to another, in tinkling fashion. And even if he culls negatives from a harsher reality in an attempt to preserve a more glorious tale, the experiences yet to emerge offer some allowances. Who would not focus on preserving the goodness and benefit of early beginnings, with the dark clouds of Nazi brutality on the horizon, waiting to bloody up the memories?

I take a breather from this idyllic storybook beginning. I picture Hollywood creating some version of this little town. Maybe they would have little girls with nice straight braids, and clean, energetic, playful boys with snakes hanging out of pockets and licorice in their fists. Still, I know we all begin somewhere, somehow, and Bennet began this way, from this place, as fairy-tale and unlikely as it seems. Bennet's life will unravel and turn into a horror story soon enough so I decide it is okay for me to float among the lovely remnants of his childhood days.

And so back into his early happiness I go.

> We were considered to be the most affluent family in the village. I went to the Czech public school as well as to Cheder—Hebrew school. The teachers at both schools were very strict. The public school teacher wielded a strong ruler, and the rabbi threatened us with a thin, pliable stick. They used objects of punishment quite often, without parental objections. We would tremble when Thursday arrived, for it was then that we had tests in Cheder. We also trembled on Saturdays, for it was then that our father tested us. We were under constant pressure, all year long. The only time for vacation was during the three-week period in the summertime, but those three weeks were a time of historical mourning in the Jewish calendar, and it was forbidden for us to swim.

Bennet's learning appetite becomes more expansive as it becomes more formalized. I smell a new quality about it, too. He is developing his own pattern of foraging for information, like an animal sniffing after food. It may be that his appetite has diminished over the years, but it strikes me more that it has likely just refocused itself on different topics, expressing itself from a different vantage point. I wonder if it has gone inside more, searching for the sense of things we don't have as much time to search for when we are younger. I imagine his mind-field to differ from others' since he has been forced to consider things unseen by the rest of us.

Our town had a little synagogue where we went to Cheder. We prayed there every morning, every afternoon, and during the holidays. We also had a ritual bathhouse, which we visited every Friday afternoon and on the holiday eves. Adults like my father would also go to the ritual bath early on Saturday mornings. Women went to the baths on Friday mornings, and also after menstruation each month (once their periods ended, they went to the bath to be cleansed).

The bathhouse was a one-room building located next to the river, for to be kosher it had to make use of fresh, living waters. One would walk down to the pool, which formed an eight foot square next to a deep stove that was heated with wood. If the water was elevated in the river due to rains, the pool would be deeper too. The stove would adjust itself according to the level of the river.

I almost drowned in the ritual bath once. I was about eight years old, and did not know how to swim. I didn't realize how deep the water was, and I walked into the pool and slipped. Luckily, my friend Nate's brother, Henyu, was in the pool too, so he stretched out his arm and pulled me up to the step. I had already swallowed some water. That's when I became determined to learn how to swim. The next chance I had, I went over to the river. No one was watching me. I swam under the water and slowly lifted up my head. That was all there was to it. Later I ran up to my friends, calling out, "I know how to swim."

Ahhhh. Practical preservation skills start early, or so it seems

# CHAPTER 5

On Friday afternoons, all work stopped. After bathing, we dressed and went to the synagogue. The synagogue was a building located across from the ritual bath, on the other side of the river. The building was divided into two sections: the main one for the men, the smaller one for the women. A long window, covered with a curtain, formed a wall for separating the sections. The old torn prayer leaves were stored in an attic upstairs. There were also two bathrooms in the back—one for the men and one for the women. I remember that there was a pitcher of water for washing hands, with a smelly towel that everybody used. There was a little porch in the front of the synagogue, and the kids would sit there, playing around, until they were old enough to read the service. If we were old enough to participate, we had to be inside.

Mother was busy all day Friday. From early morning on, she would bake challah—the twisted white bread—and all kinds of sweets: honey cake, poppy seed and cocoa cakes, cheese Danishes, and many other delicious pastries. My mother was the best cook and baker. Her food had a special taste, and we children could not and would not eat food that wasn't cooked in our home. If mother ran out of say, butter, and borrowed from the neighbor, we did not want to eat the food.

My brother David attended a Yeshiva (to study the Torah) in Bratislava, and then he went into the army. When he returned from his service, he worked with my father at the lumber mill office. He was a very capable worker. One day, Mr. Gruenberger from the nearby town of Volovets asked my father if David could join him to work in his lumber business, and he consented. Eventually, David

I wonder what quality exists in the universe that allows some to see gathering clouds ahead of the actual storm and remove themselves from its path. Bennet's siblings David and Bella sensed an emerging density of darkness on the horizon. While they likely operated from all that crackling energy of youth, they also enjoyed youth's idealism, needing to direct it towards a grand purpose. Why is the adult animal with parental responsibility the last to see? Maybe adults with families think they have more to lose. Or maybe the idea of change is too unnerving. One thing is certain: change was coming regardless, but how was Bennet's dad to know how dark those clouds were to become? Was it not obvious from what's come before?

Too many times, the man would try to use this law to extort money from the bride's parents. This sometimes happens with arranged marriages.

When I was ten years old, my father felt that I needed to receive a better education. He therefore sent Cilly and me to the Hebrew Gymnasium in Mukachevo. It was a difficult time for me. I missed my home and my mother's food. For the first year, we lived at our aunt's home in Orosveg, a suburb of Mukachevo. To get to school, we had to cross a bridge and walk about two kilometers.

Today after discussing some of his account Bennet turns, looking me full in the face. "Can you imagine a ten-year-old having to leave his home and go away for school? It is too young," he says feverishly.

"No, I cannot imagine," I say lamely. While I love to learn and I can see that Bennet is ferocious about it, it is becoming evident it has not come without a cost. It seems this is an emotional virus that has never left him. It's in his eyes. But oddly, while it caused a sense of loss in a young boy's life, it has occurred to me that Bennet may have gained something unforeseen and invaluable through this patch of time. I have a strong hunch that the boy, Benci, developed an internal fortitude that would later serve the man, Bennet, in the wretched experiences that would loom large.

"I missed my mother," he repeats. "I used to cry myself to sleep. For her."

"How long were you there, in Mukachevo?"

"Four, five years I think," he says.

Then, as if the sun has come out from under a cloud he says, "Actually Kalvin and Hudji came, too, in the beginning. Funny, I forgot that they came." His face seems mesmerized by the long buried recollection that has resurfaced.

"Huh? That is not in your original draft," I add.

"I just now remembered it," he says.

"How long have you not remembered it, Bennet?" I ask him, stunned.

"Ten years, twenty years….I don't know."

Oh dear. This has been buried a while and he obviously is moved by its unearthing. I sense a sort of sweetness in his reaction, about its resurrection. But he is quiet, and I suspect he is revisiting a piece of how he must have felt so very long ago, not to mention experiencing the sheer wonder of his retrieval of this memory.

I try to sit very still. It is hard because there is a palpable life and energy, as if a bird has lifted its wings, gaining momentum.

And then:

"By then Hudji was in her teens and came to cook for us," he continues.

"How old was Kalvin?"

"Eight, Kalvin was eight years old."

I am momentarily stalled by how young he and Kalvin both were to be sent away to another town, educational value or not, from their family. In total, four children were originally sent to Mukachevo. While the four of them likely preserved some semblance of family, the feeling of separation from siblings and parents, a mother in particular, must have been profound.

"Kalvin couldn't stay. It was too hard for him, so after about five or six months, he went home," he tells me. "Hudji stayed about a year, then went back herself, leaving just Cilly and I in Mukachevo."

After a few moments I ask, "So where did you and Cilly stay after the one year at your aunt's house?"

"Each year my father arranged and paid for us to stay in other Jewish homes. It was a tradition that the Jews would try to help each other. Then, we would take our meals at a different home from where we lived. It was called 'days' and was embarrassing. Each day we ate at a different house. Sometimes I would ring the bell where I was supposed to eat and no one would come. I would ring many times and eventually give up and go to school hungry."

There is an emotional clarity about this description that Bennet relates for me, before he adds "it was hard; it was embarrassing."

My breath has become shallow, my heart crumpling under the weight of the aloneness of a boy. He does not complain. Still, it has scraped his insides.

I know I do not know this experience of his. Bennet is telling me about a different life in a different world, in a decidedly different time. His experience cannot reach into my consciousness in the same way he lived it. I can, however, see an odd sorrow about an aspect of the experience that he has shared. I have learned you do not have to go through the same experiences to recognize the universal quality of pain when you see it. Crumpling, my heart continues having trouble bearing up under this weight.

But what's this? In a remarkable turn, I see more than sorrow on Bennet's face. His expression does not hold the one emotion. There are two. There is lightness present as well.

Oh my.

> I also developed my musical ability. I auditioned for Cantor Wolwovits at the synagogue. He invited me to join the choir, and I was even given the opportunity to sing solos. He took me under his wing, and taught me to read music. He and his wife were childless, and he even asked my father if he could adopt me. Of course, my father wouldn't even hear about this. Nonetheless, the Wolwovitses treated me as if I were their own little boy.

I picture Bennet beaming during this time. While he may have suffered from temporarily being displaced from a mother, he gained a gift of affection and learning from others—to be wanted from surrogates that provided not just caring, but an expanded sense of expression that would serve as a potent force in his life. Lovely notes on a scale, melodies, rhythm and lyrics are positioning themselves to become Bennet's first liberation of sorts. Music will begin to carry him through life's hardness, even if his mother's arms cannot.

"Want a bite?" he says, abruptly announcing it's time for lunch.

"Yes," I offer, humbly.

It is soup we end up having today, chicken soup with vegetables made by his Hungarian friend. It is simple, delicious. We are mostly quiet, except for the soft sounds of slurping. Today's lunch feels like a prayer and I am grateful beyond words, lost in the rarified air of Bennet's recent resurrection.

# CHAPTER 6

When I was in Mukachevo, I was paid 275 kronen for singing in the choir—a good sum for singing on the holidays, Saturdays, and when the new moon was blessed. Once, during the high holidays, the synagogue was filled with burning candles. I had not eaten on Yom Kippur, and the smell and heat of the candles overpowered me. I fainted, and had to be taken outside. People washed my face with cold water, and after a while I was back on the steps in front of the Holy Ark.

On Passover we would go home. Most of the time we traveled by horse and wagon—it was too expensive to travel by the bus or by the taxis that used to come from Zdenevo to Mukachevo once a week (mainly on Mondays, when the store owners shopped at the wholesale markets). When we traveled home, it would take the wagons a whole night to travel the 60 kilometers from Mukachevo to our town. We would start at 7:00 o'clock on Monday evening, and arrive Tuesday morning around 8:00 AM. It took so long because the horses had to stop twice to be fed. There is also a steep mountain along the way, where the load was heavy. An additional pair of horses was needed to reach the top. Then the extra pair would go down the hill to help the other wagons. I was always happy to go home, for I missed my mother and father and my friends. I was so young. Children today do not leave home at the age of ten.

We are developing a meeting pattern, Bennet and I. He sits on one couch in his living room, I on another, examining his life like cells under a microscope.

I ask Bennet, "How do you think this all affected you—leaving home so early, the value placed on learning, et cetera?" "I had a difficult time adjusting. I was too young to comprehend things."

"What things," I ask.

"I was too young to understand it all," he says, repeating the same notion in a slightly different way, with no further details forthcoming.

I try a different tack. "Did you like school?"

"Yes, I did. I didn't realize how important it would be until after the war, but I did like to learn."

"Do you feel it helped you in other ways?" I add.

He shrugs. "Well, sure, it made me independent. It helped me to cope with life. I learned to be responsible early."

At age ten, you learned to be responsible? I marvel to myself. It also dawns on me that he learned to be painfully alone; even with a sister present it is clear Bennet has been stripped of some of his childhood. An expanding sadness presents itself in the form of my own broken heart. If only it were possible to reach back in time and save the boy. Instead, my search is on for some salvation, some usefulness that may have come out of this educational opportunity sprung from parental deprivation.

"Do you think it might have helped you survive the camps?"

Bennet mines his answer from the depths of his own understanding when he responds "yes." He says this slowly, from a different emotional time zone, in a different rhythm, reading a more turbulent musical score.

While this Grimm fairy-tale world untangles itself, I realize it is only partly grim; it is also partly lovely. It leaks from Bennet in indescribable ways. I picture the boy growing, absorbing his environment, hungry for more than food. He is also gathering practical evidence from his life, even if he doesn't quite know what to do with the information at hand. I imagine him travelling from a town with possibilities for his future, back to a nest he never wanted to leave. I picture him innocent, earnest, eager for the essence of himself to be planted back with his mother and father. Bennet must have been pulled by a future potential, struggling against that from which he came, much like I imagine the Jewish tribe writ large, roaming around trying to find their way from a lost past to a cohesive and safer future. And I think, while this childhood experience seems punishing, how ultimately resourceful at surviving Bennet is becoming; how sad but how incredibly sweet, how incredibly reliable is the pattern developing for the patternmaker Bennet. This time in Mukachevo will serve his personal evolution well.

In the summertime, I would help the workers in our fields. In exchange for their farm work, they would receive a salary and also a warm lunch. We had no problem getting help because everyone liked our food. Hay was cut and dried, potatoes were dug from earth (without the use of machinery). Everything was performed by hand. Food had to be stored for winter. We had a big cellar for storing white beets, onions, and carrots. The workers would dig a hole in the ground, line it with straw, and fill it up with potatoes, to last until the new crop emerged. We had cows, horses, chickens, geese, and ducks. We also had a male servant, Jihnat, who was like a member of the family. Hafa helped in the kitchen, and it was her job to milk the cows.

Most of our servants were with us for many years. They would stay with us until they got married. When our servant Hafa married Fedor, who worked for us as well, my father built them a home as a present. Hafa was a wonderful girl who had even learned Yiddish and was able to say our morning prayers with us. She lived to be ninety-five years old, and after the war we would send her packages from the United States. We saw her twice when we went to visit our mother's grave in Verecke in 1988. We visited Zdenevo with great difficulty, since travel was hard during the Communist regime.

When the Hungarians occupied our part of the country, I had to quit school and move back home. I went to work with my father in the lumber business. My day began very early so that I could get everything done. I would get up in the morning when it was still dark and in the winter, I was the first to walk on the fresh snow. I was still young, and was afraid to walk in the dark from one village to the next—from our town to Zbyny and from there to Pashkivtsi, which is about six kilometers from Zdenevo. I had to walk through an uninhabited area and was terrified of wolves and bears. I'd walk with a long stick, and once in a while would whistle between my fingers to scare the animals. On moonlit nights it was bright and light, but without the moon the walk was very scary. It gets cold in that area and my face would get covered with frost. My boots would grow stiff from perspiration—that's how freezing cold it was. One time I was so frozen that I needed to thaw out. I barely made it to see a family named Lipshits. I knocked on their door and practically fell into their house. They sat me up on top of the prepichok (a raised clay oven that is heated with wood) with my feet dangling over the stove so that the ice would melt off my boots. Finally I was able to move my toes again.

My father would send me to the surrounding villages—Sherbovets, Bukovets, Perekhresnyi—to solicit workers to cut trees. A man with horses would then carry away the lumber after it was cut by handsaw into smaller pieces. We needed to break down the length of the tree to manageable size, for transporting. I would measure the length and thickness and record the numbers into a booklet. Workers got paid by the number of cubic meters they produced. The lumber was loaded onto train wagons and taken to Svalyava by a small locomotive. Usually, four people loaded the wagons—two on each end. We used a special tool to push up the lumber, and if a worker failed to show up, I would be the fourth one to help with the job. It was hard work to push large pieces of lumber onto the train—one worker would give a signal, and everyone would push simultaneously.

I would bring my lunch to work. It consisted of bread, eggs, onion, cheese, and a bottle of tea with lemon (many times it would freeze and would have to be put near the fire to thaw—sometimes the bottle would crack and ruin the drink). We'd start the fire around 11:00, so that by noon we were able to bake potatoes. The workers would take a piece of bacon, put it on a stick, and twirl it in the fire to let it drip on the potatoes or on the bread. Sometimes I would do the same thing with the fat bottom of a goose or duck after it had been force-fed.

At the end of the day I would sometimes get a ride on the train or on the sled that the horses pulled. Bells would jingle around their necks as they trotted. In the evenings, I would help father figure out how much each worker had earned, based on the cubic meter calculations. After a while I remembered the numbers, so I would not have to look up the value of pi. I remember being so tired, nearly asleep as I would tell my father the numbers. In the mornings, my boots were sometimes still damp from the day before. My hand-knit socks were thick and not very dry. But I had no choice. Even so, I would often cry in the mornings, wondering when life would get better. I would sing to cheer myself up. I remembered some of the solos that I had sung when I was a choirboy. I would sing them to pass dull times.

Another day, I am at Bennet's. We are in the back room, his nest for working Sudoku puzzles and monitoring world events. The news is on the television and there is talk of workers demonstrating at the G-20 economic summit in London. Both police and demonstrators have been injured. "A demonstrator has died," says the announcer.

"Did you hear that Bennet? A demonstrator has died due to injuries sustained from police," I tell him.

"They should work; they should be working," he says gruffly, as he turns away from the screen, a sour look penetrating his face. "If the protesters don't like the way the world is, then why don't they try to make it better? And not by breaking windows and devastating property—let them use the energy to work hard and be productive."

"But you do believe in their right to demonstrate, yes?" I ask him.

"Of course, of course," he says. "It's one of the things I love about America, and other countries like it. Where I come from you couldn't do this. They just shouldn't be violent."

While these events unfold in London, with some people feeling great economic injustice due to a global meltdown, it is also quite clear to me that Bennet's point comes from somewhere deep in the Carpathians. I see frost on his face now, but coming from the slow freeze of a child's exhaustion whose bittersweet memory has never quite left. I see wet socks still half frozen. I see hands being rubbed over and over in an attempt to thaw them. I cannot escape the fate of a boy who learned early—too early—you work or you don't survive in the world.

And you do what, so you don't die on the inside?

You sing. You better sing.

# CHAPTER 7

Today, Bennet and I are back on our favorite perches. He is on the couch facing the window, always looking out at the world. I am on the couch perpendicular to his, always watching him.

Life under Hungarian rule was very hard. One day, father was dragged to the police station and beaten up for no reason—for being Jewish. As a boy, this was painful for me, to see this happen to my father. There was nothing we could do. The Hungarians were barbaric, not very educated. They had to show everyone that they were the big conquerors. In 1937, before the occupation, Cilly and I were attending school in Mukachevo, Shary was divorced and living back home, Esty was running a bar, and Hudji had married a dentist named Nachum Strobel and was living in Verecke. Kalvin and Shimi (Steve) attended public school in Zdenevo.

I used to worry about Steve. He was several years younger and I remember trying to look out for him when we were playing. So when I was at home, I would try to keep track of him, make sure nothing happened. That year, Mother became very ill. She was taken to a hospital in Mukachevo—the large city in our region, and the only one with a hospital—where she was diagnosed with meningitis.

The doctors tried to cure her, but to no avail. She was not going to live much longer. Mother told Dad that she wished to die at home, in her own bed. Around February 10, 1937, she went by ambulance, with Cilly and me, back to Zdenevo. It was winter, and the ambulance could not reach our village, so Dad rented horses and a sled for the final stretch to our home. Mother was in great pain, and we did all we could to make her comfortable. I would bring her lemonade and went to her bedside every few moments. On the morning of February 14th, she called my Dad, telling him that up until then Benci had given her the pleasure of cups of lemonade, her favorite drink, and now, for the last time, Dad should give her the lemonade. A few moments later, she passed on.

The whole village came to her funeral. Mother had been unique, her hands always open to anyone who needed help. We were devastated, especially the three youngest children. Steve and Kalvin were preteens, and I was in my midteens. Mother had worked very hard in the store while my Father worked at the lumberyard. She also had tended to the kitchen and the servants, making sure that the field workers had lunches. And she had taken care of her own mother, who lived with my uncle Saul and his wife Ziesel, who had no children of their own. (Ziesel eventually survived the concentration camps and moved to Israel after their liberation. I visited her whenever I traveled to Israel, where she made the best garlic toast; one could smell it all around her apartment.)

I still remember how I would play on the floor when my mother was resting on a bed in the living room, after doing her work. She would ask me to take off her shoes, and I still have the scent of her feet in me. It was a soft odor, and I remember the black stockings she wore. We all loved her so very much. Even now when I meet someone who mentions his or her own mother, I say, "Take good care of her." Unfortunately, Aryeh, David, and Bella could not come to her funeral. Jewish law says that the burial has to take place as soon as possible. The day after she died, her body was placed on a sled, with a pair of horses, and she was buried in Verecke—about twelve kilometers from Zdenevo—at the Jewish cemetery. We cried constantly. We had lost the best mother in the world. I still think of how this loss has affected all of us throughout our lives. We did not know anybody else who had lost a mother so young.

"So your mother was hospitalized in Mukachevo, the town where you and Cilly were attending school. Then you returned home for her final days. How long was that?"

"About two weeks," he tells me, staring back.

All is quiet in Bennet's house now, so very quiet. I think about my own mother's death, she in her eighties, and even though I was forty-seven years old when she passed, I felt orphaned. Bennet was so very young to lose a mother, not once, but twice, since he was denied her daily care once he left home at age ten to go to school in Mukachevo.

"I still smell her feet; it's in my system," he has told me.

Of course. If you can smell it, you are breathing it in; by definition, inhalation is taking it into your system, so Bennet's statement has not just his own validation that is transmitted out of his face and eyes, but also that of the material world—science, I suppose. His exhalation of her is in his memory, in the kindnesses she taught him, not here in form maybe, but certainly in spirit.

There is something else, too, that I know with the most remarkable certitude. A mother's love knows no death. I see Bennet carry her with him each day. Oh, this may not always be conscious for him. Rather, it is the kind of carriage that reveals itself in his reverence for life. I see it expressed in his devotion to his own children, his siblings, and his family at large.

Bennet tells me of the anniversary of her passing, that each year he goes to temple, lights a candle in her honor, and says prayers on her behalf. Ironically, I see no contradiction in this loving act of his, not believing in a formal notion of God maybe, yet praying nonetheless. No, what I see is his devotion to a love that knows no death, operating both inside and out of time. It is a force greater than himself, boundless and infinite. Name it what you like. As Elizabeth Stone once said, "….to have a child is to decide forever to have your heart go walking around outside your body." I know this as a mother myself. On some occasions when he has spoken of her, I have tried to imagine how she might have felt as she lay dying, as she contemplated leaving her brood to the perils of the world without benefit of her continued shepherding. The thought overwhelms me.

So what I see Bennet doing is walking around with the scent of his mother incorporated in his own living. He honors her each time he is generous, giving, and compassionate. She was his first guardian, shaping his personality in that most powerful of ways, loving him through his early days. How fortunate I am to witness some of her kindness and compassion revealing itself in Bennet, extending her influence and spirit forward in time.

And I know that the loss of her actual life was profound for him. Two weeks at home after your mother has died at such a tender age? I can hardly bear it. How did he bear it? It occurs to me he has lost an anchor. It also occurs to me, however, that he has preserved her—as a rudder with which to navigate events that are to come. It is evident in how he has chosen to live his life. I once asked Bennet what was the best day of his life, and the worst day of his life. You know what he told me? Best day: "liberation." Worst day: "my mother's death." She is imprinted in the chambers of his heart.

Sadly, at the time of her death, all predictability in his environment at large was disintegrating at a rapid rate as the winds of change gained momentum.

Cilly and I went back to school. But the situation was not calm there. Life was upset, not just in our home but for all the Jewish people. Soon the Hungarians arrived with an authoritative and ruling presence. Business transactions were difficult, and father was forced to get a Gentile partner, a man named Ivan Sxobran. The lumber mill ceased to operate. The Hungarians dismantled the machinery and moved it to Svalyava. Many families were deprived of their livelihood.

Shary, Esty, and Cilly moved to Budapest. After a while I came to help father in Zdenevo. After school, Kalvin learned to sew, and the girls took Steve to Budapest. Hudji's husband then was deported to a Hungarian labor camp and he never returned. People who had seen him told us that he had frozen to death somewhere in the Ukraine, where the Germans had forced him and others to dig ditches and perform hard labor. Hudji had a beautiful little girl and they came to stay with Dad and me.

After a while my Father did not like not having a wife. About two years after mother died, he married a widow in our village. However, the marriage lasted only a short time before they got divorced. I don't know the reason for their discontent. People then started to recommend other widows, and my father soon married a woman—also named Mermelstein, but not a relation—from Nelipino, a town about 30 kilometers from Zdenevo. She had four children. We did not really care for her. She didn't cook or bake like our own mother. And we didn't like the idea of having a stepmother.

They were married until they were taken to the brick factory ghetto in Mukachevo, and from there to Auschwitz, where they were gassed with Hudji, her baby, and my grandmother, my mother's mother, who was then in her eighties.

Bennet was so young to endure the enormity of events in his life. They say heaven and hell is only a tenth of an inch apart. Already, Bennet has known such loss and sadness. How can it be that the worst is yet to come? The gap will be measured in a thousandth of an inch, or less, far closer to hell than anything else.

■

Watch a man in times of … adversity to discover what kind of man he is; for then at last words of truth are drawn from the depths of his heart, and the mask is torn off.

*—Lucretius*

# CHAPTER 8

I t is another day at Bennet's; another session.

"I don't believe in God." He has just volunteered this out of the cosmos. It seems to be the Gospel According to Bennet, his own religion of sorts, spreading his commitment to his notion of non-God.

"No God. There are billions of stars....how do you call it...in the Milky Way—fifty percent of the universe. No one knows how they got there. No God up there. The Milky Way is awesome, beautiful. I love nature," he says, impassioned. I can see his connection with nature rising out of him, like steam off a lake. But it is clear to me that God has been banned from his world, excommunicated like the heretics of the Middle Ages, interfering with ideas, no, interfering with his perception of his experience.

He turns serious, "People asked me for help in the camps; 'Benci'—my given name—'help me,' but I could do nothing. God did nothing. How could He let this happen?" he spits my way with a small amount of firepower.

It seems his logic operates in circles and I am unable to respond further, feeling no answer of mine would satisfy him. While my own notion of divinity is quite different, additional discussion will be tabled for now. Bennet has firewalled God, defined him in terms I cannot touch. The post-camp man—while not straying far from the Jewish traditions of his childhood training—has clearly drawn a line in the sand with respect to the God aspect of his past. What I have come to understand about the human experience with all its subjective curiosities is that it is always answered on an individual basis. One person doesn't get to decide for another. I have not walked on his blistered and bloodied feet, so I will respect his right to a private non-God.

But the Jewish man Bennet came from childhood Benci beginnings; he tells me of his early life in a cultural ecosystem that up until now, for me, has come only from books or movies. It seems I have been naïve all along. Not to the knowledge of the pre-war events themselves, of course. Rather, my naïveté has been based on shallow assumptions about the human component—what it might have been like to live and breathe (and die) in the Holocaust environment, as well as in the times leading up to it.

I look down at the account he has written about that time, desperate to make sense of the events, their meaning.

> At the age of seventeen, I reported to the Hungarian authorities. All Jewish boys were forced to sign up for labor camp, while Gentile boys were sent to the army. I was sent somewhere near the Romanian border. By a fortunate accident, I met my best friend Moishe Wolf there. He was a year older than I. I also discovered another good friend from Zdenevo, Nathan Davidowitch.

Bennet shares with me that he doesn't believe in destiny either, so of course his view of meeting Moishe is "a fortunate accident." For one who doesn't believe in destiny, he is to have many fortunate accidents in his life to come. The gods are conspiring on Bennet's behalf, or so it seems to me.

> I also remember a boy who took care of the pigs and chickens in camp. He too was from a village in the Carpathian region. When I moved to Los Angeles after the war, I recognized him at a charity dinner. His name was Sam Reese, and he had lived in Canada before settling in California, where he was in the jewelry business (in fact, he made my Masonic ring). He never married, passed on in 1990, and had a sister in Israel.

"You don't believe in destiny? And you just see this man in a crowd that you knew decades ago in a tiny area occupied by the Hungarian army, in a labor camp you once shared?" I ask, incredulous but believing.

"Nope," he says firmly, digging in.

Ha! I'm starting to put his accidents and coincidences in an imaginary box. I ask Bennet if we can argue about this later. He says "well, okay," sheepish-like. For now, my attention keeps being drawn to his story, what he has written in the downward spiral of his account.

Life was no picnic. We were assigned to work, building a big airfield. Our job was to pick up little rocks and form pyramid-shaped piles. We were required to complete a certain number of piles. After we met our quota, we would help other workers who were not strong enough. The Hungarian guards were rough and uneducated. They would punish us at any opportunity and made our lives miserable. Sometimes they would make us write something hundreds of times. Sometimes the punishment was physical. They hanged prisoners by their hands pulled behind their back, feet dangling off the ground. Or they would make someone crouch down holding a broom in place behind their knees, sometimes for a half hour, sometimes longer.

Our barracks were up on a hill, and twice a day we had to push a wagon with a barrel to the river. We would fill the barrel with water, since the camp had no piped-in water and the primitive toilet facilities were all the way in the back of the camp.

After the labor camp, we were sent to Borgond, near Szekesfehervar, a city southwest of Budapest. We were put up on a farm near an airport used by the Germans. Life did not get easier there. I was assigned the care of sixty horses that worked on the airfield. Nate helped me. I also remember a racehorse named Hansi, whom the Germans had brought from Poland. My job was to tend to her, feed her, and groom her. If anything bad happened to her, it was my responsibility. In the beginning, I could not even get close to her because she would kick and jump. I could barely feed her, and grooming was impossible.

Slowly, however, she began to recognize me. I was the only one that really got close to her.

Eventually, Hansi let me ride her bareback. She did not permit the sergeant to do this, and this frustrated him. Whenever an air raid occurred, we had to tie the horses up in pairs and get away from the airport. Of course, I would jump on Hansi and gallop away as fast as I could. At noon one day, the alarm sounded. I immediately jumped onto Hansi and rode off to the cornfield. All of a sudden I saw a plane aiming in my direction, shooting "ra-tat-tat." The noise was horrid. I jumped off the horse and fell to the ground. However, Hansi ran away. I was terrified that she had been hit, and that this would mean the end for me. Trembling, I rose to my feet. The planes had flown off, so I walked to a little elevation to look for the horse.

Suddenly, I saw her, shaking her head up and down. I was relieved that at least she was alive. What could I do? I whistled through my fingers, and sure enough, she saw me and waited. As I walked toward her, I called, "Hansi, Hansi," just to calm her down. When I got hold of her, I noticed a bruise on her back, right where I had been sitting on her. A bullet had strafed her back there. Had I not gotten off her, I would have been shot in the thigh.

I asked the Ukrainian veterinarian to attend to her, but not to tell my sergeant. He cleaned up the injury, put salve on it, and covered Hansi with a blanket. That day, the English planes had killed two horses.

Life was hard. There was constant pressure, and we hardly got to sleep at night because of horrible conditions, hard slats to sleep on and cold, always cold. Eventually my friend Nate and I decided to escape to Budapest. The sergeant, however, almost shot Nate. He was caught speaking to a Yugoslavian girl who was visiting her brother—a civilian worker for the project. The sergeant was furious that Nate, a Jew, was talking to an Aryan girl. It was not allowed. A Jewish man could not speak to a Gentile woman. I was terrified when the sergeant threatened Nate, so I ran to the sergeant's girlfriend, who was a beautiful Ukrainian with whom he lived. I begged her not to allow the sergeant to kill my friend. The sergeant still took the gun out of his holster, but because he was drunk—he was always drunk—it misfired and Nate was saved.

Am I witnessing a peacemaker here?

"How long were you in this camp?" I wonder out loud to him.

"About two years," he says.

But of course besides Nate not getting shot, an even more miraculous event is about to unfold.

> Finally, one night we escaped the camp. It had been a horrendous place. We had to tolerate constant harassment, yelling, hard work, primitive conditions, and huge lice that never left us alone. They crawled anywhere that there was hair: in the head, under the arms, and in the crotch. I would go to the outhouse to pick them off. But the process was useless. They were all over, sucking out the little blood we had. Never in my life had I seen such big lice.

I look up from my notes, staring at Bennet.

"How did you escape exactly? You write that you got a fake ID by trading shoes and just left. How did you do it? You make it sound like crossing the street, that easy even."

"It wasn't too hard," he tells me. "It was a labor camp and there was no gate. Even though they had guards there weren't that many. We just snuck out at night in the dark."

"If it wasn't that difficult, why hadn't you done it before that night? Why did you do it at this particular time?" I'm still wondering out loud to him.

"Well, Hungary was having a lot of, how do I say it, commotion in the country, so we knew it would be an easier time of it," he says.

"What kind of commotion?"

"The government, it was unstable. There was political commotion and unrest," he reiterates.

"How old were you then?"

"About twenty."

> When we escaped, we walked at night and hid in the bush during the daytime. I had an identification certificate that I had bought from a Yugoslav for a pair

of boots, which Shary had brought when she was able to visit me once at the railroad station in Borgond. The ID said that I was a Yugoslav working in a factory in Hungary. One night as we walked, we saw a truck that had a flat tire. We offered to help the driver fix it on condition that he take us to Budapest. The driver went as far as Buda and we sat with a group of Hungarians who constantly cursed the Jews. Had they known that we, too, were Jewish, they would have thrown us off the truck.

We arrived in Buda early in the morning, and walked to the Chain Bridge to cross to Pest. Soldiers guarded the bridge, and they asked for our papers. I showed them my ID and I crossed the bridge with Nate right behind me. I went immediately to Shary's apartment to see if I could hide there. However, the police showed up there so often that it was too dangerous. I would have put everyone in danger since I was an escapee from a labor camp.

Bennet also tells me that at this time he was trying to find a friend who was part of the underground, hoping he would be able to hide him. His name was Henyu, but Henyu was not to be found. Bennet's hopes dropped like overripe fruit falling to the earth with a very heavy thud.

Eventually I was caught on the street and put into an army barrack with hundreds of other young and old Jews. Little did I know that my brother Kalvin was there, too. They had picked him up on the street. I had only been there about four days when I saw him suddenly—by accident—at the other end of the large barrack. I was both happy and sad. He was just a young kid, about seventeen, and had no idea of what was happening. He planned a daring escape, but I was afraid that he would get killed. I vowed that we would stay together so that I could take care of him.

In the here and now, I ask Bennet, "Why did you still get picked up if you had the fake ID?"

"Because I was a Jew," he says flatly.

The Jew was not just persecuted, but had no rights. You didn't have to do anything. It was about what you were.

I ask Bennet, "You escaped from the labor camp, why not this camp?"

"The Hungarian labor camp was different," he tells me. "This camp was run for the Germans. We were told anyone caught escaping would be killed. I was afraid Kalvin would be killed."

"So the possible cost of failure was too great," I query him.

"That's right. It wasn't like before."

After a few days, they took us to the railroad station and loaded us into cattle cars. We found out that we were going to Germany. The cattle car was filled to capacity, with no room to turn. We were crammed like sardines, with waste and urine all over us. When the train stopped outside a station, the half-dead and sick were pushed out. Yet even in the wagons we speculated that most probably we would work on farms, taking care of animals. It wouldn't be so bad, we thought. But as soon as we arrived at the station in Oranienburg concentration camp, the big doors opened and we heard screaming, both from the prisoners and from the Germans. The SS had big dogs and sticks. As we ran down the ramp, they hit us and pushed us in all directions. I could not believe that people could handle other human beings in such a brutal way.

We had to empty all our pockets and place our bags and possessions onto a big pile. I had a razor compact, a ring, a thin necklace, and Tefillin—the phylacteries that Jews put on the head and the arm when they pray in the morning. I had carried them with me everywhere. They were small enough to fit into my pocket. They were supposed to be treated with respect, but I had to throw them on the ground.

We were marched to a big hall, forced to undress completely, and sprayed with some kind of disinfectant. Then we were given our numbers inked onto our arms. Mine was 109827, Moishe Wolf's was 109828, and Kalvin's was 109829, given that way because of how we were lined up. We were given prison outfits—striped uniforms and shoes with wooden soles. It was the day we lost our identities as human beings. We stayed only for a few days.

Oranienburg was the first concentration camp for Bennet. I learn that Oranienburg was originally built in 1933, early in the Nazi regime, holding political prisoners from the Berlin area mostly, but also numerous other kinds of detainees as well. It was situated at first in the middle of town (by the same name) so that anyone could see into many areas of the camp. I try to imagine average German citizens going about their business, gazing over and quite possibly witnessing people being not just held, but also being brutalized periodically. At its largest capacity, it held about three thousand prisoners. While operating, many prisoners performed forced labor on projects in the town.

After a few days we were loaded onto trucks and taken at night to a concentration camp in Ohrdruf. By "we," I mean Kalvin, Moishe Wolf, and myself. There were many others, but I didn't know their names.

We were put into two-tiered barracks, the floors of which were lined with straw. Early in the morning, the SS forced us up, screaming "RAUS, RAUS," which means "OUT." We were forced to line up for counting. Our numbers had to be exact. If by chance someone was missing, we had to wait outside, no matter how long it took to locate the missing person. Every morning we were loaded onto trucks and taken to different types of work areas. We were nearly starving. They gave us black coffee, consisting more of chicory than coffee, and a piece of very hard bread, the size of two small slices. No food was distributed at the work area, unless we could find scraps in the garbage. I remember finding a half-eaten apple, and how I appreciated it. After working ten or twelve hour days, we were given another piece of bread and a bowl of soup. If there was a potato peel in it, I considered myself lucky.

Ohrdruf was built in 1944 near Weimar, Germany. At its peak it held nearly twelve thousand prisoners. Bennet was in Ohrdruf for the better part of a year, a much longer tenure than other locations where he was held. It was to be the home of continued forced labor for him, moving rocks, digging trenches and ditches. Ohrdruf was part of the Nazi effort to extend the railway project and was a sub-camp of Buchenwald.

I sit heavy on the couch, there is so much gravity pulling me into the enormous density of Bennet's story. How do words, even though they are the carriers of potent, dramatic, and profound facts and feelings, truly convey his experience? I imagine them to go only part way, and even though I've been hungry before, never for days, weeks, or months. I've even been afraid for my life before, but never for several years straight and certainly not under these kinds of conditions. To sustain a level of terror and keep going in the face of it is something foreign to me. This cannot help but alter how you see the world, for benefit or for ill, and probably a combination of both. I do not have to know the depths of this experience to believe it rearranges your insides, your head and thinking, so that they are never to be the same.

Never.

■

# CHAPTER 9

We would return to the barracks each night, and this is the way my life went on for months and months. Eventually we were taken to another camp, located in Crawinkel—I don't even know how to find the place on a map. At this new camp we stayed in bunker-type huts; their shape was round, and inside we found the same two-tiered housing. In the center of the huts was a stove that we tried to keep burning, but wood was available only if we could bring it from the work area.

Crawinkel camp was located northeast of Frankfurt, southwest of Berlin. There does not seem to be a lot of information on the camp but it was known to have huts, forced labor and a quarry. It likely served as one of the many transit camps in Germany, besides the forced labor program.

Finally I had the idea of collecting pieces of wood to hide under my blanket. I had a large piece of cloth—remnants from a coat—that I wrapped around myself. To keep warm, I would tie a rope around my waist. This piece of cloth was large enough to hide the pieces of wood that I took.

The wood could not be seen by the guards or by stronger prisoners who might think of stealing it. After we finished our soup, I would go to the cooks to sell the bundles of wood for a good bowl of soup or for a few cigarettes. I would bring the type of can that had been issued to all of us, and I would fill it with the soup that was on the bottom of the big pot. This way, I was able partly to fill my appetite with vegetables. I would take my spoon, Kalvin would take his, and we would share our new soup. I would usually let him have more than I'd had, because he was not too strong. Kalvin had diarrhea and that is fatal in camp, so I took some bark from a tree and boiled it in water and gave the tea for him to drink. Fortunately it helped and he got better. I wish I knew what type of tree it was.

I tried to exchange wood for food or other goods as often as possible. The cooks needed the wood for burning in the barracks. Soon I had an established clientele who waited for me to bring them the heating material. In time, other prisoners had the same sales idea, and they too were able to sell wood, mostly for cigarettes.

How resourceful, I am thinking. What an entrepreneur. Sometimes out of horrifying situations, ingenuity spontaneously erupts. I might even imagine he recaptured some sense of personal power, however tiny it may have been, and something else: could it be hope?

I suspect this hope, however, is tenuously balanced against a nearly ever-present idea of non-survival. Six million Jews were sent to their deaths while approximately a hundred thousand survived. Most of the former literally went up in smoke. One of the latter sits in front of me. The tension between living and dying sometimes balanced precariously on a piece of wood or a potato. While Bennet's context is large in the historical scheme of things, the content of his experience is smaller, subjective, and personal.

He is framed in a piece of cloth held together by rope. There is a mesmerizing quality about knowing someone who has survived; the potency of the experience compressed in human flesh feels more powerful to me than the totality of the Holocaust itself. It reminds me of quantum theory—the smallest quantity of radiant energy, sudden and significant, erupting into manifestation, moving feverishly, appearing visible and large. The pressure to keep life in motion had to have been profound. And here it sits, perched on a couch across from me.

Can you imagine? I hear him whisper, as if from a dreamy fog. The Holocaust has penetrated him, planting itself inside the nucleus, the RNA of his cellular structure. How does one remove that from their experience? It is the virus that never leaves.

"I had a friend who used to load bodies for burning for the gas chambers. In Auschwitz," Bennet has told me.

But you collected wood to stay alive. It is like parallel universes.

The following day, I cannot help but think of fire: fire and Bennet. It is fire season in Southern California and its timing could not be more eerie. This morning there is ash on cars, the sidewalk; it is everywhere with numerous flecks floating in the air. I try to imagine Bennet witnessing a different kind of ash, knowing it came from his people, his tribe. There is a quality I cannot get to. Then, as if he has pulled me back in time, I look out of eyes that are not mine but provide vision nonetheless. For a moment I see the camps and through inhalation I am breathing Bennet in, as if he had come from the ovens himself. It is oppressive and hard for me to walk, with my well-fed constitution and comfortable lifestyle. It is as if the weight of the ash that I am breathing is measured in tonnage, the air so thick that I must push it out of my way in order to continue.

How does it happen? How exactly does one carry on in the face of massive madness? The bridge is narrow and precarious, a thread that for some snaps quickly but for Bennet holds firm. Some sense of mission or purpose propelled him into his future. Bennet was smart, is smart, so he used the resources at his disposal, not the least of which was his cunning, shrewdness, wits, and instinct. But there is also Kalvin.

Besides hope, there is the prospect of duty, devotion, something larger than Bennet operating. There is love for a brother weaker than he, a brother who needs his help if he is to survive. Bennet is his brother's keeper. His heart beats not just for one, but for two.

When I return from my walk, Bennet's account is there to greet me, as if to say "this is only the beginning." At once I know that I gasp not just from ash in California air. I also need to gather more oxygen for what is yet to come.

One day, Kalvin and I were assigned work in the stone quarry. I always wanted him to work with me so that I could help him. On the truck ride to this assignment, I cautioned Kalvin not to speak in Yiddish. When he asked why, I implored him just to watch out, because in the quarry the capos and Ukrainian guards sometimes would take a Jew, just for fun, and throw them down the rocky hill to be killed. I gave the same advice to a Hungarian Jew who was a doctor. The Hungarian did not believe me. Before long, he was one of three Jews to be thrown down the hill.

On that day, which turned out to be a German holiday, the capo came around with a pad, asking everyone his name. When he questioned me, I replied by stating only my number, 109827. The capo asked for my real name, to which I replied, "Rjashko, Ivan." He asked for my nationality, and I answered, "I am a Ukrainian from Czechoslovakia." Then he asked in Ukrainian to test my language skills—and I was lucky, because I spoke it well. Then the capo moved on to Kalvin. I told the man that Kalvin's name was "Rjashko, Vasely, my brother." Fortunately, he did not test Kalvin, because my brother did not speak Ukrainian well.

Because of the holiday, we were each given a cigarette, but at the end of the day we had to carry three bodies back to camp because everyone had to be accounted for, whether they were dead or alive. The numbers who left in the morning had to return at the end of the day.

Episodes like these were frequent. But being inquisitive and aware of our surroundings saved us from a lot of horrible times. So often I saw people die, get sick, cry, beg for help, and receive no help. The odds of survival were truly against us.

My best friend, Moishe Wolf, was a smart boy, a year older than I was. He was the only boy in a family of nine children, and we had been the best of friends since I had been just three years old. We had been together until I was sent to Mukachevo to school. One day, in the camp, we dug ditches together and prayed. He quoted the prayers and I repeated the words after him. We wondered, "Where was the Great Helper?" Where was the One who was supposed to protect us from evil and suffering? Where was he now? All we saw around us were older men and young children being wasted to skin and bone. People covered with open blisters and wounds, bleeding from their mouths, barely able to utter a word. Together we walked over dead bodies that supposedly had been created in the image of the Almighty. Now these people could not even get to their final resting-place in dignity. Men who supposedly were also created by the same Almighty were treating them worse than animals at the slaughterhouse. Where was justice? Where was the dignity of mankind? Where was compassion and feeling?

Of course, I don't possess an answer that will satisfy Bennet. Man's animal behavior seems tangled with man's prescribed behavior of God. The Book of Job says "there is a spirit in mankind." From where I sit fifty years later, I still hear Bennet's and Moishe's echo: "Where is the Great Helper?" I know where He is: He resides in part in Bennet, poured into him so that he may reach others with his story.

Without a doubt Bennet would scoff at this. He is a literal man. Differing ideas of God are a disagreement he and I are to have for months. Yet, the glimpse of something beyond the literal man presents itself. That something, that spirit rests in his actions. It is the squirrel he feeds. It is the turtles he cares for. It is the tiny flower poking its head out of the ground in springtime. It is the rainbow arching from Buchenwald to Beverly Hills. It is the ash that has found its way into my lungs, to be exhaled out onto the page.

I had been lucky. I had been born into a nice home, with good food. The mountains were beautiful, the fresh air so healthy. My past helped me to endure such misery and hardship during those hard times. One day I saw a man from our village. His family, like mine, had run a general store. He was tall and had flat feet. When we were kids we used to comment on his noticeable frame. His name was Josef Leib, the son of the "tall Abraham," as opposed to another Abraham who had been short. In the camp I was sickened to see how terrible he looked. The tall man was now shriveled, bent over, barely able to walk or talk. Finally he died.

But of course, this is not the end.

# CHAPTER 10

Bennet has come back from visiting his sister, Cilly, in Israel. "Everyone should see it. It is so beautiful there, green and lush," he tells me, his face blissful. Today we are in his nest in the back, the den, rustic pine panels on the walls, even the vaulted ceiling, similar to his home in Zdenevo.

Bennet is nearly reclining on the couch we both share, his eyes alive. He sits on one end, I am on the other, as if we both need to anchor it. "How was your sister," I ask, but he seems to evade the question. Finally, after I ask several times, he says, "She is frustrated, has trouble with hearing, her back hurts, it's difficult to walk.

"What time is it?" he says, looking quickly at the clock. "I'll call her."

He rings her up, speaking rapidly in Yiddish, his voice raising several pitches. I hear her through the phone. Her voice has the energy I would imagine someone related to Bennet might have, much like his own. I try to picture a little Cilly, as the child that went with him to Mukachevo, the two of them huddling together, bonding in a particular way that children must when a family emotional support system has been stripped away. Oddly, I hear both versions of her: Cilly then and a seventy-years-later Cilly now, a fusion for sure of siblinghood that Bennet shares uniquely with her. His affection sits on the couch between us, robust as the voice I hear coming through the phone. It is lovely to witness, to be sure, palpable and real, infusing the room. It is as real as the light coming through the sliding glass window, although is not subject to scientific measurement in the same way.

"All the people in Israel have been very affected by the child who has been orphaned from the killings in Mumbai, India," he tells me after hanging up. "Cilly has felt bad the last few days since the killings, as the parents' bodies have come back into the country."

At once I feel a pull between Bennet and Cilly's past experience of being hunted, trapped, confined, abused because of their Jewishness and the present events that have happened just last week. An extremist Pakistani group has killed 195 people, many Indians, some Americans, Brits, and Jews, although it is the Indians the extremists were after and, sadly, the Jewish family were innocents in the way. Still, the seventy-year-old thread connecting Bennet and Cilly's past with the Nazis serves as a fuse. Any form of extremism now electrifies their previous experience, flashing back and forth on a white hot continuum. I imagine, too, that the entire Jewish identification of persecution, while possibly blunted with age and maturity, has never entirely left. After all, how on earth could one forget? Tangled, potent and transferrable, the Holocaust penetrates into current events.

And maybe the point is not to forget, although it is likely important to put things in constantly updated perspectives.

"Can you ever imagine yourself not being Jewish?" I ask.

"No," he says, shaking his head, slow but deliberate.

We move to the dining room where Bennet has a waist-high fireplace. There is a great fire going. It produces about as much heat as the energy system that Bennet himself creates. Oh, dear.

"I love fires. I love the warmth," he growls happily. We stay long enough for him to warm his hands, before moving back to the couch in the den.

Remarkably, Bennet steers the conversation to another topic; he starts talking about forgiveness. He tells me there is a Jewish tradition that during the High Holy Days, ending on Yom Kippur, you are to ask people in your life for their forgiveness of something you may have done to them. I like this idea and tell him so.

"I try to tell my children that if I have done something wrong, I am sorry," he says. He repeats this. I think this notion has become more and more important to him these days and I am wondering why, exactly, this is on his mind.

Forgiveness is a topic that I am particularly sensitive to, having made many mistakes that have impacted others negatively. After all, who hasn't made them? While I want to forgive others' errors because of how exonerating it feels, I want to be forgiven as well. I like the breakdown of the word: 'for—give—ness'—two separate words really, that mean for giving; to give.

I look up at Bennet and say, "I went through about nine months of asking my son to forgive me for things I felt responsible for in his childhood. My son tells me he has."

The clear eyes of Bennet stare back at me. He nods some understanding but stays private with his thoughts, hidden like so many peanuts his squirrel has buried across the street.

How utterly interesting the mood is now. The room is thick with unsaid stuff; thick!

"I went to a funeral recently, my second cousin's," he offers. "We have a Jewish tradition at funerals where you ask the dead person to forgive you for anything you might have done to them."

We talk about how some people in our lives have trouble saying "I'm sorry" or times when we ourselves have trouble doing the saying.

Bennet returns to silence. Clocks are ticking in the room, waiting.

"I think for some people it is very hard to own up to their flaws," I tell him. "It's as if they are handicapped and, while they are still accountable for errors they've made, they are not able to take responsibility for them. It has been hard for me at times, and still is on certain subjects or with certain people," I add. "So I try to be as patient with others as I want them to be with me."

He seems to be considering this. Another slight nod suggests that this might be true for him as well, but I can't be sure.

Oddly, this conversation has taken on a life of its own, probably for both of us. "Sometimes I am so embarrassed, in front of myself, how I have behaved, the mistakes I have made," I confess helplessly.

And then he says, "I shudder sometimes at some of the things I've done."

My posture seems to be correcting itself as I lean into his thinly veiled confession.

"But don't you think it's great when anyone can see that they've made a mistake?" I ask him. "Not just because a person can take responsibility for their actions but because they can see the error at all. A person can then change, growing from the awareness, and forgive themselves," I continue. "It's like giving back your own innocence. After all, a mistake is an error, a behavior in time, not the essence of a person."

Remarkably, I remember the bread story. Bennet's cousin told the rabbi he stole from another inmate when he was in the camps and cried with great remorse, years after the fact, feeling bereft, but also freed by the telling. The animal wants to stay alive. His cousin was trying to stay alive. The horror of the behavior, I suspect, was the knowledge that the man he stole it from could have died from not having that last piece of bread. Do I pick me to stay alive? Do I pick him?

Plus, I am deeply struck by the likelihood of things unsaid that all of us carry, whether or not they are shared with another as the Jewish tradition suggests. To even acknowledge in one's own interior is a healthy thing, a redeeming thing. I suspect Bennet might share this sentiment himself.

My serial queries to him reverberate back to me: "Have you forgiven the Germans?" His response: "You can't stay mad at an entire nation." This, of course is true enough, but still begs the question. How hard it must be to release all that anger, shame, and rage. Does it go inside, get transmuted, and come out sideways in different ways, transferred to other targets?

I have told Bennet of a small story in my past, of having my husband taken as a political prisoner while we were in Iran. I have told him how angry I was—for decades. My husband was jailed for a month and while I, too, was trapped in Iran unable to leave, Bennet was imprisoned in one way or another for three and a half years, by Hungarians first but more brutally by the Germans, for being Jewish.

No, you cannot stay mad at an entire nation but that doesn't mean trauma doesn't change your being, or how you see the world. Of course, to stay angry or to swallow it, will damage you in untold ways, burrowing deep, becoming harder to identify and correct.

With these thoughts I sit up straighter on my end of the couch and redirect my perspective to smaller sins.

Of course it goes without saying, I am incredibly curious about what things Bennet regrets, but will not press this. Maybe another day; maybe never—it really doesn't matter to me. It matters to him. For the time being, there seems to be redemption present in this conversation, and maybe that is why he brought up forgiveness at all. It is remarkable not only to watch a Holocaust survivor reflect on horrors that loomed large in his life as a victim, but also to examine smaller infractions committed by one's own self. Obvious as it may seem, I have learned that size is a relative thing determined by the role and perspective of the viewer.

Yet for him, I wonder what the man struggles with, along with the other hundreds of thousands of Holocaust survivors. How distorted do some perceptions remain while others are freed from the cycle of victim and perpetrator? How do the sins committed in war infest marriages, parenting, citizenship, relationships? It seems forgiveness may be the final step to true liberation, no matter the circumstance, no matter the size of the infraction.

By necessity, forgiveness is the ultimate release, the ultimate liberation. Why else has Bennet brought this up?

■

# CHAPTER 11

An announcement filled the camp one day. Anyone who knew how to sew was asked to report to the office. Kalvin had learned to sew in Zdenevo, so we thought that this was an opportunity for him to work inside. Surely mending military clothes would be an easier task than moving rocks or digging ditches. Kalvin reported to the office, and soon got the assignment to repair military and prison officials' clothing. He did this for quite a long time, though I cannot recollect exactly how long. One day, however, I returned from work and could not find him. I panicked, and soon found out that a new camp had been created. I learned where they were expected to line up, and in the morning I went to look for him. Sure enough, I tracked him down, and when I finished my work I went to his place.

By this time, I think it must have been around February 1945, we had heard that the Americans and British were not very far away. The Germans started to move us because they didn't want the Allies to find us. I was afraid that Kalvin would get lost because he was at the other sub-camp where he did sewing. They loaded us from both camps in trains, wanting to move us deeper into Germany. But the Allied planes used to come and strafe the trains with bullets. As a matter of fact, I got shrapnel in my thigh and Kalvin got a bruise on the nose from bullets and shrapnel. A Hungarian man that was sitting between us got killed.

Because of the attacks by the Allied planes, the locomotives were knocked out and we got back to marching. We numbered in the thousands and I had become separated from Kalvin. At one point we were stopped in an open field;

> there were many of us from numerous camps in the area. I had a feeling that Kalvin must be close, so I stood up on a tree stump and called out "KALVIN! KALVIN!" but got no answer. After a while I did it again and sure enough I saw someone waving from afar and right away I recognized him and started to run towards him and we were united.

I am at Bennet's the following day, after reading this remarkable turn of events from his account. "There were thousands of prisoners and you find Kalvin? Don't you think that's incredible?"

"Yes," he says. But there's an itch in him. It's coming from the inside somewhere. He is squirming on his couch in the living room, unable to sit still.

Then I notice something else. The light from his front window is falling differently on his face and Bennet's atoms have rearranged themselves yet again. What comes out of his mouth next is as remarkable as what has preceded it from the account. Bennet proceeds to tell me that his friend Nate, who now lives in New Jersey, has called him within the last few months. Nate has told him that while he rarely goes to synagogue for services, he has gone recently. The rabbi at this synagogue that Nate hardly ever attends is giving his talk and is describing some miraculous events of the Holocaust. The rabbi tells of two brothers—Bennet and Kalvin—who had gotten separated during the war. They were on a death march with thousands of other Jewish deportees. Bennet, of course, was worried about his younger brother as always, but particularly since they had gotten separated.

The rabbi proceeds to describe the events of Bennet finding Kalvin, standing on a stump, calling his name, and seeing his brother's hand go up, miraculously. They are reunited. Nate tells the rabbi after services that he knows them both, that he grew up with Bennet and Kalvin, went through some of the war with them. Nate asks the rabbi if he, too, knows Bennet and Kalvin Mermel?

"No," says the rabbi.

"How did you hear about their story then?" asks Nate, incredulous.

"Well, once when I went to the Holocaust Museum in Washington, D.C. I watched Bennet's oral history video of his experiences, and this story stood out. I've always remembered it," says the rabbi.

"Nate called and told you his experience with the rabbi in the last month or so?" I ask Bennet, stunned.

"Yes."

I watch Bennet closely now, as he finishes this tale for my consumption. He is excited and happy. I can see it on his face. It is the kind of happy that works its way from somewhere deep, a kind of "this is as it should be" thing, natural, organic even, uncontrollably emanating from his eyes and smile. It is utter joy, pure and satisfied.

Later, I repeat this remarkable tale, this series of scenes, to my son. "Do you understand what all had to happen, Mom, to reach this point? Thread it backwards," he says. "Nate had to go to the synagogue he rarely goes to. The rabbi had to talk about Bennet and Kalvin that day. The rabbi had to have gone to the Holocaust Museum in Washington, D.C. While at the Museum, the rabbi had to have seen that particular oral history—out of 20,000 histories—zeroing in on that particular scene. Before that, Bennet had to have been taped by Steven Spielberg's people fourteen years ago. Bennet had to have had the original events with his brother during the war. Not to mention, he had to know Nate. It is fantastic," says my son. "And, you have to know Bennet and be writing his memoir for you to even hear it."

"Yes," I say. Time has slowed now as I am seriously struck by it all, by Bennet's confluence of events, by Bennet's "paying it forward" to impact others, to inspire, not just me but the rabbi, Nate, and even Bennet himself maybe. After all, it has come full circle; the very act that he and his brother lived out has come back to Bennet, but shared with an even larger audience, like adding water to an already full river that overflows it's bank, ever-reaching. Bennet gets to be both participant and witness to himself. Is there a force larger than Bennet, larger than all of us, conspiring on Bennet's behalf?

I wonder.

In the evening, I return to Bennet's account.

While we were marching I carried a rucksack for a German SS and he was a nice guy and sometimes gave me cigarettes and sometimes bread. So when Kalvin and I met, I had all these goodies. I called my friends, Moishe Wolf and a boy from Verecke, I think he was a watchmaker, and we covered ourselves with the blanket. I started to divide the bread. Within seconds other prisoners jumped us and tried to take away the bread. They stepped on my hand and broke the skin and I was able to salvage half of the bread, and we allowed ourselves to smoke one cigarette amongst ourselves.

The weather was very bad. There was a cold rain, and we were stuck in a field outside a village. Moishe Wolf was so weak that he could hardly talk. When he dragged his feet, his legs were so stiff that they could not bend at the knees. He looked as if he were walking on stilts. His nose was plugged up, and he was very thin. Of course, we were all skinny, with eyebrows practically hanging in our eyes, but Moishe Wolf looked like what we had come to call a "Muselmann"—the term we used when someone was horribly emaciated—the walking dead. An announcement ordered anyone who could not walk to wait in the field. We were told that horses and wagons would come from the village to take these people to our destination. Little did I know that these people would be shot, and that the villagers would bury them right there. Only later did I find out that my best friend had been shot and killed, along with fifty or sixty others.

Of course, I hoped that Kalvin and I would survive. But I was uncertain when I saw our group dwindling from weakness as we marched from place to place. The Germans did not want us to be captured by the Allies, who were closing in on them from all sides, so we marched and marched, though mainly only in the late afternoons.

One day, Kalvin threw himself down in the gutter and said that he did not want to live any longer. An SS officer quickly pointed a rifle at him, ready to shoot. I grabbed Kalvin and pleaded with him, saying, "You see the light there in the distance? That's where we are going." I got our friend Gyula Glantz to help me drag Kalvin, which he gladly did because I had shared my bread with him.

As we passed through a village one evening, the townspeople gave us potatoes. I managed to receive two potatoes, and Kalvin got one. That was quite a treat, for we had not eaten in days. On another evening, we were sent to stay at a farm, and we went to sleep on the hay. We dug ourselves in deep so that we could stay warm and dry. Kalvin and I had considered hiding there, but thought it was too dangerous. In the morning we were awakened by the Nazis jabbing long wires into the hay to see if anyone was hiding. A few prisoners did manage to hide and escape.

Next we went to Flossenburg concentration camp and stayed there for a few days. After much more marching we went to Buchenwald. We were at Buchenwald for several weeks. While there, I met my cousin, Melvin Mermelstein.

Flossenburg was built in 1938 in Bavaria. More than ninety-six thousand prisoners passed through Flossenburg while it was under operation. Again, there was a quarry. It also had a large labor contingent and a crematorium.

Buchenwald was known as one of the most brutal camps in the German system. Buchenwald opened its doors in 1937, operating as a labor/concentration camp until liberation in 1945. Interning more than two hundred fifty thousand prisoners, it was one of the largest in Germany. It was one of the camps where human medical experimentations were conducted

After the several weeks' stay at Buchenwald, Kalvin and I were forced to march again because the Allies were getting closer. Finally we arrived at the Bavarian forest. We had started off numbering in the thousands from several camps, but in the end we were just a few hundred prisoners. Many either dropped dead along the way or, if they were too weak, the Nazis shot them where they dropped. As was common, people from local villages would come by afterwards, pick up the corpses and bury them.

I put Bennet's pages down and look away, pulling at the corners. His story is carried in words when there are no words to convey this devastation, this degradation. Human beings not being human; they are not even behaving according to nature. Bennet and Kalvin are adrift in a sea of misery never before known on this magnitude. In my heart of hearts, it remains unfathomable. Facts about individual camps' size and location convey little information regarding the suffering contained therein. Wooden slats to sleep on, huts, and quarries have no beating hearts.

■

# CHAPTER 12

I continued to have terrible headaches, which had started back in Ohrdruf. They had started there when I had gone to an officer to plead for shoes (my feet were wrapped with rags). The SS man hit me on the head with an iron pipe in response to my request (my head is still dented from the blow). Later, as I stood in the Bavarian forest—called Stamsriederwald—I heard the noises of tanks and trucks, but had no idea what the sounds meant. At the time, I thought they must be the Germans. Then, all of a sudden, I saw the SS men stepping to the side of the prisoners and changing into civilian clothes. I whispered to Kalvin that if they didn't shoot us right then, we might live.

Suddenly, I fainted and fell. We were near a river and my face went down into the stream. Kalvin shook me and washed my face with cold water, so I woke up again. Since we were alone, I told Kalvin we should run down the hill to get away. This whole time I felt like I was in a trance. We saw a farm down the hill and hid in the outhouse. We were afraid to let anyone see us, and we had a tense time because people tried to enter the outhouse. One woman in particular was persistent, banging on the door. The outhouse was small, maybe three feet by six feet, with one hole and a board off to the side. Kalvin and I had to share the cramped space, room only for him to sit and me to stand. We were frightened but excited—two brothers trying to hang on. Of course, there was a stench and we did not know what was happening outside.

We thought that the tanks and trucks belonged to the Germans and could hear they were coming close as the noise got louder. But then I heard a woman shouting from a second-floor window to her next-door neighbor: "Die

Amerikaner sind hier."—The Americans are here. I peered out through a crack in the door, seeing her with one eye closed, squinting. When I heard these joyous words, we emerged from our hiding place. That was the first time that we saw a black person. The American soldiers had arrived.

How subtle is Bennet's description of liberation, the best day of his life, by his own admission. In fact, it may have happened just this way: one day you are prisoner, the next day you are free. The turning, while seemingly easy, has its own powerful pivot, throwing you off kilter, into a whole new universe, one filled with uncontainable joy mixed with sorrow for those not to have escaped death. Also there is something new: the awareness of what you've survived hitting you full force, leaving you in a truly altered state of being, unprepared to live a new life.

There remains a surreal quality about liberation. Another day, when Bennet and I are meeting he says, "I'll never forget the shock of it. It was almost unbelievable, like a trance."

There is a tension captives hold inside themselves. The longer the captivity, the greater the tension that one contains, wrapped tight. No way can Bennet or Kalvin just release it all just by opening an outhouse door—not after three and a half years of keeping it in place.

"Overall, you were in five or six camps, yes?" I ask, trying the impossible, to tally up the damage.

"Yes," he tells me, adding "we marched for periods of time between camps. Some were very short stays, a few days—like transits—sometimes we were in camps for several weeks. Mostly, I was in three that were longer, six months or more."

Is the man a collection of his experiences? Or is the man a collection of his insights gained from his experiences? I wonder. Always, there is the literalness of an event to which our animal self responds, trying to stay alive with as much dignity as possible, sometimes having to stretch what dignity even means. But, of course, there is also the interior experience, usually only lived later, when one has the luxury of being able to process it, to think on what it means, how it felt beyond the raw fear.

In addition, because a person usually thinks about the same experience over time, one's perception, knowledge, interpretation beyond the distortion or fading of the linear memory, necessarily changes. I wonder how this has played for Bennet. He doesn't remember, or at least not share, a lot of details. Some survivors can speak to the length and ferocity of a beating. Others can describe in infinite detail the scope of their daily lives in the camps, the stench, the degradation, the translucent skin pulled over skulls. Not Bennet. Rather, he weaves just enough detail to form cloth used to create a garment designed with beliefs about life and the living, certain values, and what he wants to tell others about conclusions he may have arrived at from it all. It is no wonder he became a patternmaker. His focus is on the pattern made manifest in form, its ultimate outcome, its final consequence.

How has his interior thought about his Holocaust experience evolved? No one can know for sure, not even he. There is a chill in the air, though, as I recall his statement made earlier to me: "There are things I've told no one." I am witness to the difference in Bennet when he displays straightforward energy revealing things remembered, as opposed to the slumped-shouldered posture that he carries in an effort to contain that residual tension from captivity, keeping the horror just out of sight.

Author Pema Chodron says that "usually we think that brave people have no fear. The truth is that they are intimate with fear," which is to say, when the suffering gets so overwhelming, they are able to become intimate with it, depersonalize it somehow, and ultimately, transcend it. I see this in Bennet. I see it. There is a quality, a drive if you will, that is evidenced in him, a life force so strong made up of composite material in his spirit and psyche. He can feel certain kinds of fear and move beyond it. But never can he tell it all. There is no language for certain things, I don't care how many languages a person knows.

The Americans threw us chocolate, candy, and bread. We were elated to see them, though it was hard to convince ourselves that this was not a dream. We could not jump for joy, however, because we were very weak. The Americans installed a kitchen in the middle of the village. They gave us food and army boots. We could barely walk. It was April 4, 1945.

But we got sick from eating so many sweets. After four days of feasting, Kalvin developed a high fever. I took him to the American army hospital, where he was diagnosed with typhus. I was told to leave him there, that I could not remain near him. This was too much for me to take. Crying, I implored that I had saved his life and had carried him all over. Why would I have to leave him here? I was able to speak a little English, having studied it at the Hebrew Gymnasium in Mukachevo, so the doctor explained to me that typhus was contagious.

I walked back to the village—its name was Cham, in the Bavarian mountains—where I stayed with some prisoners in an empty house. I was extremely despondent. After two days, I, too, grew very ill. With a bad headache and a fever, I barely made it to the hospital. The same doctor who had diagnosed Kalvin told me that I had meningitis, and he assigned me to another section of the hospital. My disease was also contagious. I was terrified. My mother had died of meningitis. However, the doctor assured me that penicillin would cure me. He explained that when my mother had been ill, this cure had not yet been discovered.

The hospital was overcrowded, so I had to lie on an army cot on the floor in the hallway. After a while, I heard coughing and somehow sensed that it was coming from Kalvin. I tried to scream out his name, "Kalvin, Kalvin," but he couldn't hear me; I wasn't calling loud enough. When a nurse walked by, I asked her to see if by chance a boy named Kalvin Mermelstein was in the next room. She told me she didn't have the time to check for things like that, so I stopped the next person who walked by, begging him to see if my brother was nearby. He was more helpful, and sure enough came out of the room, saying, "Yes, it is him." I begged him to tell my brother that I was there, too, and he did convey this message to Kalvin. We were told that we could not see each other because our illnesses were still contagious.

After a day or so, I was put into a room by myself, given injections of thousands of units of penicillin, and made to drink whole cans of water every few hours. After about two weeks, I started to feel better, and the conditions in the hospital had quieted down a bit. As I remember now, this hospital was filled with sick young men and women. Some were American soldiers, but the majority consisted of prisoners who had survived.

I told the attending physician how Kalvin and I had survived the terrible times, and how I had watched over him, often taking less for myself so that he could have a little more food. And now, after all we had done to stay together, I couldn't even see him or determine if he was alive. I asked the doctor to check on his condition.

Of course, there were no telephones in the rooms, so I could not even arrange to call him. I hoped that Kalvin was still alive. All of a sudden, the door opened and there was the doctor wheeling my brother in just a bit, just enough for me to see him. We both began to cry out of happiness, thrilled that we were alive and still together. After three more weeks we were released from the hospital, still weak and shaky, and we were taken to a convalescent home to recuperate and regain our strength.

I think of the American hospital in Germany, to a recovering Bennet and Kalvin, crying and laughing at the discovery of each other's presence. Everything in their lives is gone. The thread connecting to anything remotely ordinary, at least initially, is only one another. Quite simply, each brother is the other's life raft.

How does Bennet do ordinary from here?

■

# CHAPTER 13

Both of us were very thin. I was not even able to sit comfortably on a bench because my frame consisted of skin and bones. My eyes had sunk deep into my skull, with my eyebrows sagging over my eyes. My teeth were loose, and I could not chew anything that was hard. I went over to a dental school to see if my teeth could be saved, and was lucky to find an elderly dentist who gave me hope about treatment. He said the procedure would be very painful, however. I said, "Okay. I can stand the pain." I was hoping to avoid the fate of one of my acquaintances, a man named Krool who had come from Poland, played the piano, and came from a family of cantors. He had to lose all of his teeth. I endured painful vitamin injections into my gums. The needles were thick and the procedure hurt badly. But the dentist saved my teeth, and they remain in good shape even today.

Kalvin and I stayed in the convalescent home for four weeks. We both were mostly recovered from our illnesses but still very weak. The surroundings, next to a little lake, were beautiful, and we would sit by the water. When we got stronger, we walked around the lake. The staff was very nice and they made sure we ate well, so we could gain some weight. They also gave us clothing. When we felt even stronger, we decided to go to Hungary to see if anyone from our family was still alive. Right after the war, the trains did not run very often. Schedules were confused, and many of the train stations had been bombed out in the total chaos. Most trains and trolleys were free because of all the chaos and people who were dislocated. We finally boarded a train toward Budapest. When we arrived, we searched for Rumbach Street, where Shary used to live.

We found the remains of the building—it had been bombed and was in shambles. Then we walked to Esty's apartment house, on Furst Sandor Street. The structure had survived. We found the apartment, left of the entry hall, and we read a note on the door that said, "We are in the basement washing laundry."

When we saw this note, we were overjoyed. We rushed down the stairs, opened the basement door, and experienced the happiest moments of our lives. We screamed, cried, and yelled with joy so much that the residents of the building came rushing down to see what was happening. Some people thought that the Russians were attacking someone in the basement. Russians did not have a very good reputation.

Bennet sits on his perch on the couch, clear-eyed as usual. After all he has been through, it is remarkable to me that he has written this down like so much story, something that has happened with other characters. He describes being happy, ecstatic even, upon seeing his sisters, but there is a quality, too, that is laced throughout, that is un-relatable for lay people who have no personal knowledge of siblings or parents lost. There are no words in the eight languages Bennet knows to convey his joy, their joy upon discovery of the living. It is an emotion lost in translation.

The girls had no idea that we were going to show up at that time. Someone, in fact, had reported seeing us lying dead in the gutter. Nonetheless, my sisters had not given up complete hope. All three of them—Shary, Esty, and Cilly—were still alive. I asked about our brother Steve and was told that he would return in a few days. I was skeptical about this reply, for I had spent my childhood worrying about Steve, especially on Saturdays when we would gather by age groups. He was younger and smaller and I felt protective of him. My sisters assured me that he had gone on a business trip to sell cigarettes. This was one object that could be sold for a profit. I learned later he was selling them in Zdenevo on the black market. Then, he would get food from Zdenevo to bring back and sell in Budapest.

After some of the excitement, the girls undressed us and gave us a warm bath and food. They could not believe how skinny we were—how could we have survived? Soon our joy was reduced, however. Saving the worst news for last, the girls told us that our father, sister Hudji, and Hudji's baby had all been gassed in Auschwitz.

Stop. Three individual deaths of the six million. Can you imagine? One of Bennet's favorite phrases reverberates in my skull, but this time it hurts. My chest tightens. Take these three and multiply the pain quotient, the emotional confusion of surviving, and you have trauma of staggering proportions swirling in a psyche. No, Bennet, no. I cannot imagine—all the wounded walking around. Some will immigrate to America, some to Australia, Britain, some remain in Europe. The fierce survivors? They will go to Israel. All of the Jews spreading throughout the world will carry not just their individual fractured memories, but a collective one, culminating in a screaming prayer: Don't let this near annihilation of us happen again. It is an unresolved tension that plays out in the Middle East still.

But I've gotten ahead of the story.

My sisters survived in Budapest by pretending that they were citizens of another country. They worked in a hospital as aides, doing all kinds of dirty work. One day, Cilly was caught and captured by the police. They suspected she was Jewish and took her to the border, preparing to send her to a camp in Germany. A Hungarian farmer allowed her to make a telephone call, and she was able to reach Shary at the hospital. She pleaded with Shary to send someone to rescue her, and Shary gave some jewelry to an SS officer, who arrived just in time to save her from being deported to Germany. Cilly arrived back in Budapest and returned to work at the hospital when it was safe.

"What was day to day life like after the war? How did you eat, get clothes, and get around?"

"As I said, it was chaotic. There was lots of black market activity for ordinary goods. There wasn't always reliable distribution like before so individuals would locate items people needed, buy them, and then sell them to customers. Like what Steve did with the cigarettes and food. Also, items were more expensive in the few stores that were open."

"So it's not so much that products were contraband. It's more like the system was broken. Is that correct?"

"Yes. And the girls helped us. They were working and Esty was married so they helped us too. And there were Jewish organizations that helped. They would provide used clothing, food, things like that."

"So you rested and recovered more in Budapest, with your sisters. Then what did you do?" I ask.

"After about five or six weeks I wanted to go home to Zdenevo and see how things were there, even though Father was dead and no one was there," he tells me. "Kalvin stayed in Budapest with the girls but I made my way to our old house. We had hidden some things before the war: silver, candelabra, and gold plates from my brother-in-law's dental practice. They were hidden under floor boards in a shed and behind a false window from the cellar where we kept wood," he tells me.

"There were three families living in our house. One was our former shoe polisher. I discovered all the items were gone. The town was already under Russian control and there was a man, Fedor, who patrolled the town with a gun. I told Fedor I wanted our things."

"Do you want to make trouble?" Fedor asked Bennet. "Do you want to go to Siberia?"

"Of course I was scared, I did not want to be taken away again so I went to a neighbor lady's house and stayed that night. I woke around three in the morning to sneak out of town. I walked about ten to fifteen miles to a train station. After the war the trains were unpredictable because of all the bombing. I finally made it to a station and went back to Budapest."

"How long had you been in Zdenevo?" I ask him.

"About a day," he says. "I was afraid to stay. Everything was gone. There was nothing to stay for," he tells me, shrugging his shoulders.

There was nothing.

I realize I don't know anything about having nothing.

We are eating lunch: fish out of a jar—Jewish food. Bennet is quiet. He is looking away from me much of the time, against the backdrop of clock ticks and soft swallowing sounds. He is private, self-contained.

You want to look inside a life that has known such things as gas chambers, fractured families, rebuilding from nothingness? The surviving siblings in Budapest are standing in the middle of an intersection, their emotional and psychic engines temporarily stalled. This is the picture in my mind as I look at Bennet not looking at me. There are nine known survivors of his immediate family, three having gone to Israel before the war, three sisters and a brother having hidden during most of the war—in plain sight, I might add—Bennet and Kalvin having survived the camps and marches.

You think they're all lucky? Blessed? Yes, of course. Of course, with so many of them alive. But make no mistake about it. The Mermelstein family—and all Holocaust Jews—have a very different definition of ground zero. You have to learn how to survive freedom. You have to fit some less-than-attractive but very practical survival skills into a new circumstance. To survive the war they all had to hide certain things: identities, feelings, names, languages, to name a few. Learning to withhold information protects a person during the crisis, but also after. It is confusing to those of us who've not known extreme containment. Things can come out sideways. Sometimes it comes out in anger, resentments.

But sometimes it can come out in a song.

■

# CHAPTER 14

Kalvin and I stayed at Esty's apartment much of the time, and sometimes we stayed at Shary's place. Esty's husband, Odon, was a highly educated person with a good position as the director of the Anglo-Hungarian Bank in Budapest. He used to take us to concerts, which I loved. I listened to all kinds of music on the radio and knew that I wanted to study music. Hungary was fast becoming communistic, a satellite of Russia. I concluded that there was no future for me there.

About six months later I decided to go to Czechoslovakia to Usti Nad Labem. It is north of Prague about one hour's drive. Being a refugee, a stateless person, I was given an apartment that had been abandoned by a German family. After the war, the government provided housing for people who had been displaced and met certain criteria. It had two bedrooms, living room, and kitchen. Eventually Kalvin and Steve came, too, and we lived together. When friends came to the city and did not have a place to stay, they stayed with us. There were two girls from Orosveg (the daughters of the ritual rabbi); when I lived in Orosveg I used to play in their yard, so when they came to the city they stayed with us until they went to Germany. We kept in touch long after the war. One now lives in Israel, and the other in Baltimore.

I was looking to make some money, and since I knew the lumber business, I got a job with Eugene Newman who was from Zbyny, about three kilometers from Zdenevo. Many times Kalvin and I used to go on Saturday to pray there in a little room in their house because you need ten men to make a quorum to be able to pray, and there were very few Jews in those villages so they needed a few boys that are thirteen years old at least.

I worked there for a while but I could see that the Russians were practically taking over the country, and Communism was taking hold. I started to tell everybody that we could not stay, and asked who wanted to come with me to Germany. I had a girlfriend that I met while in Usti. Her name was Maria. She was a teacher and came from Prague. Once we went by train to her home in Prague for a weekend; that was the first time that I saw the beautiful city of Prague. When I told her that I wanted to go to Germany, she was sad, and even though I hated to leave, I saw the writing on the wall: Communism is taking over the country. After discovering I could get help through the War Reparations program, one day I simply gathered up my few things. Some of my clothes were still damp from washing. I went to the station and boarded a train that was leaving for Germany. I had very little that I had saved from the war—things like chewing tobacco that the Germans would distribute to prisoners. I carried no identification, and once the train started moving, I tossed all of my belongings out of the window. I didn't want the police to know who I was. In the end, this was silly of me, because one could really travel anywhere without a ticket then.

Finally I arrived in Munich. But where was I to go? I asked where I could find a displaced persons' camp (DP Camp), and was told to go to a place called Frieheim. I took the trolley—I think it was the number 6—and found the camp. It was an old army barrack that was not divided into women's and men's sections. We were all homeless, and the authorities supplied us with food.

In the camp, I met my cousin Ludwig Teichman, who was my mother's brother's son who ultimately immigrated to Australia with his brother, Jack. Many of the people were waiting for their relatives to bring them to the United States or to any other country that would take them in. I, however, did not have any relatives in the States.

Because I wanted to study singing, I found out about the Handel conservatory on Mohl Street. I got up my courage and approached it. In the office, a woman asked me if she could help. I told her that I wanted to study music, especially voice training. Speaking a decent German, I told her where I was from and that I had been in the camps. I said that I had been in choirs since the age of eight and that I already knew how to read music, and that my father had always wanted me to sing. She was sympathetic and arranged an audition for me with the rector of the school. I was in my early twenties at this time.

Speechless; yes I am speechless. How could Bennet go to Munich after the war, after all the Germans did to his life?

"How did you do this, go to Germany?" I ask.

He squirms on his couch and looking up, simply says "I wanted to study music, like I said."

Not satisfied, I ask, "But why there?"

"It was possible to go there; there were some opportunities."

I take a breath and ask my serial question: "Do you feel like you've forgiven the Germans?"

More squirming. "There are good people and bad people. There are good Germans and there are bad Germans. Besides, you cannot hate a whole nation."

Of course this sounds so logical, so Bennet, but also off key, a bit flat. It does not hit the center of the note.

I'm waiting on the couch, desperate to practice my own self-control, which is not easy for me.

Then suddenly it spills out: "At that time I wished I could meet the man who beat me up and beat him up" he tells me, soberly. "I don't think I could have done it though," he adds, finally. "But I was that mad." Remarkably, he emits the smallest of laughs at himself.

If Bennet had run into the man on the street, could he have beaten him? I don't see it. Anger and rage, yes, but even sixty-five years later, he does not hold the kind of interior in evidence that could do such a thing. In his words, "there are good people and bad people" and it doesn't seem possible that, given the choice, Bennet could have committed this kind of violence, even in his youth, even after all the brutality he had endured. In self-defense, maybe if permitted he is likely to hold that instinct and act on it, but not in retribution. I just don't see it.

This is the Bennet I see: *I used to sing to cheer myself up* when he was a small child in Zdenevo. His earlier statement permeates his experience: when he used to help his father in the lumber business, in the cold, keeping the lions, tigers, and bears away in the dark of night, just like in the Wizard of Oz. It seems Bennet carries not just the comfort of music, but the power of it into his new life. It is to become an engine, fueled by his secret self, his very nature maybe, gently leading him back from the darkness, into the light and over the rainbow. Bennet is fluent in the language of music—the language of peace that replaces the war he has just survived. Music, of course, also has the benefit of singing rage out of the soul.

The day of my audition I was so nervous that I had a diarrhea attack from the anticipation. I arrived early and waited in the lobby. They called me in, finally, and I entered the room. The rector of the school was seated at the piano, and he was with two other men and a woman. They asked me to choose a song to sing. I didn't know any classical music, not having heard an opera before Odon had taken me to one in Budapest. I only knew songs that we had sung at home on winter evenings, as well as a few Hebrew tunes that I remembered from the Gymnasium. I asked if it were suitable for me to sing in Hebrew. They said 'yes,' so I sang a cappella. I sang a song called "Veulai." They wanted to hear more, so next I sang a Yiddish song, "Vee Aheen Sol Ich Gehn," and they seemed impressed. I had come from the Carpathian Mountains, lived through concentration camps, and still wanted to study.

I told them that I was living and eating at a DP camp. They talked among themselves, and after their consultation told me that I was accepted at the school. They asked me to return the next day, to discuss my situation and schedule. I was jumping for joy when I returned to the camp that night.

The sun has come out from the clouds. Rancid potatoes in thin broth are about to be replaced by nutrient notes. Move over, Don Quixote,

Bennet is on the move. The man may be short in stature but he is long in guts. He has taken his courage to Munich!

# CHAPTER 15

When I arrived at the conservatory the next day, the secretary informed me that I would not have to pay tuition. Of course, payment would have been impossible for me. I didn't have a pfennig in my pocket. Eventually they found me a room with a German family and I was able to start school.

Meanwhile, Steve was able to get on an English transport to London. Due to his alertness, and with help from Kalvin on the medical exam, he was able to go on a program for a few hundred orphans in England. Kalvin too had arrived in Munich, shortly after I arrived. He was taken to another Displaced Persons camp in Wasserburg. There he met many youngsters who had lived in our area of Europe. I would visit them on weekends—and I would have a few decent meals there.

The children under the age of seventeen were taken from Wasserburg to Prien, a beautiful area next to a lake and a castle. Eventually the JOINT, a Jewish charity organization, got families in America to sponsor them to come to the United States.

Bennet has been going through some of his boxes of items from the past. When I arrive this morning, he is all excitement incarnate and sizzling. There is a small booklet in his hands, papers that are gray from years of storage.

"These are notes I took when I was studying in Munich. I couldn't afford the books so I wrote everything down that the teacher said. It's all in German. I taught myself," he says.

"Taught yourself?"

I leaf through the pages. The script is tiny, very tiny, I assume so he can fit more on a page. Each one is filled to capacity. It is clear to me that Bennet had not just an appetite for the singing of music but also for the learning of it, the structure, and the rules governing how it functions. Even without my knowing German, the studiousness of his effort is obvious. I think of the Sudoku or word puzzles he works these days and realize how fastidious the man is about exercising his brain, putting it to use with the best of intentions, even back then. Especially back then.

Of course what I still cannot shake is his efforts to pursue a life in Germany. He could have become a bitter, angry man after what he endured. He could have chosen such a different course. Many others did. What does Bennet do in response to such a young life filled with tragedy? He goes to the former lion's den. He just gets on with things. Remarkably too, Kalvin follows him. Kalvin could have stayed in Budapest, with the sisters. But Kalvin, of course, cannot remove himself for long from the rarefied air of Bennet—at least not yet.

I am reminded of that bile that carried desire to find the man who beat him so mercilessly. Is Bennet looking around corners for the man's face? Do certain streets in Munich draw his gaze with him hoping to find his tormentor? Does he have another hidden agenda in Munich? Regardless of lingering impulses, it is clear the path Bennet is choosing at this time. His larger impulse is to preserve life, not just his own and that of his kin. More importantly, I see the thread sturdy and sure that is to carry his respect for all life channeled into a communication device that connects, not divides.

I think, too, of political extremism that Bennet and I have talked about for hours over the last several months, a painful and touchy topic to be sure. After all, extremist thinking was to fuel the birth of fascism and Bennet has gone to its source. That source has robbed him of family and friends and stolen a homeland. It also has left residual fear, operating like radar, about mankind's worst impulses. But here's the thing that is so stupefying from where I sit on Bennet's couch: he has made the choice to unmortify his experience whether he knows it consciously or not. It must have been a very tricky time for him but clearly one he had designs to master.

This is no small feat. The phoenix rising from its ashes springs forth and I am witness to a man whose face appears on the head of the bird, flapping his wings as he seeks to be airborne much like the notes he sings. Bennet operates from his better nature in that most invincible of ways. Greek myth has it that one "tear from the phoenix's eyes can temporarily make someone immune to death, regenerating when hurt or wounded by a foe."

Wounds he has but regeneration is in the offing. All I know is here sits Bennet, the phoenix exhaling his life across the continents. His tenacity for living in the most dogged of ways is remarkable. It is at once quiet but not quiet. His actions have volume, crescendo even. Is it true that he thinks nothing of what he perceives as the most logical of decisions in this choice he has made? He presents his story to me as if he were doing something quite simple, like chewing gum or eating ice cream, taking a stroll—as if it were all that predictable and ordinary.

"I just wanted to sing." Does he not know the inspiration his actions present to others? Does he not know that the courage to inhale German air and exhale it out in notes is electrifying? The nobility of music is to trump all the degradation of his concentration camp past. Ironically, he is to be in Germany almost the same amount of time he spent in the camps. Ultimately, his time there is to fuel far more than the individual man. It is to fuel others, and for a long time to come.

"I hated the Germans while I was in camp," he tells me. "But afterwards, while I know some of them knew what was happening, the population, what could they have done? You know General Eisenhower made some of the townspeople bury the bodies after the war, made them see what happened. He also made sure there were plenty of pictures taken so the world would not forget."

"Don't you think, too, that facing your past and offering forgiveness is its own liberation?" I ask him. Of course forgiveness is no easy task.

"Hmmm," he emits, considering this. He seems to be busy inside his own head.

*You can't hate a whole nation* reverberates in my skull. It does not mean Germany will not be held accountable, of course, but Bennet's uncanny ability to seek in its soil his own personal compensation is inescapable. In the most phenomenal of ways, it seems he has reached into the German womb to retrieve and regenerate an essential part of his essence, in an unconscious effort to liberate himself yet again.

In 1947, after having studied at the conservatory for one year, I took the entrance examination for the Academy of Music, and was accepted with a scholarship. By then, the institute had a special kitchen for Jewish students to have lunch, and I had moved to another home, on Schelling Street, not far from the university. I lived in a large room with a porch, and my landlady's name was Miss Schmidt. She was an older spinster with a heart condition that turned her face perpetually blue. She was perpetually waiting for her brother to return from the war but to no avail.

She ignored me in the beginning. The housing authority had assigned me to her, and she was not very happy about this. However, after a few weeks she determined that I was well behaved, and she began to talk to me. Eventually we became friends. She also allowed me to use her kitchen to heat up canned food that I received from the JOINT.

Fraulein Schmidt was very interested in theories of Extra Sensory Perception, and told me that I emitted a good aura. I would accompany her to lectures on the subject. However, she began to intrude on my personal life. If a girlfriend were visiting me, she would get quite upset. She'd walk around slamming doors shut, and walking in the hallway to let me know that she was around. It was her theory that the girls were trying to rob me of my good aura. I am sure that she never had a loving relationship with anyone, not even with her parents and certainly not with a man.

"So what do you think about ESP?" I ask.

"I learned a lot about it when Ms. Schmidt took me to the lectures. I believe we all have auras, that we emit certain powers," he tells me.

"Like energy?"

"OK, maybe."

"I think so, too," I confirm. "I think we are all in a sea of light, of energy."

"Yes," he says settling into the idea of it. "I can tell when I will get along with someone, like a woman, or when I can't. You feel it. You cannot be taught," he adds.

"But Ms. Schmidt took you to the lectures. Weren't you taught?" I ask.

"I was taught about it and then I knew how to feel it. It was always there; I just didn't know how to understand it. The lectures taught me that," he clarifies. "You know the halos painted around the heads of holy people are auras. That's what they represent," says Bennet, always the teacher.

"I guess I never thought of it that way. Of course," I say.

"Do you ever think about how you think?" I ask.

"What do you mean?"

"I mean do you think about the way you think? The way you make connections?"

He seems perplexed, stumped even. "I think and then I do," he says.

Aha! I have given him a puzzle he cannot answer. How fun.

I think and then I do. I snort to myself, I'll say.

I picture him on Mohlstrasse, on his way to his Handel Conservatory. The whole school is situated in one building. He has told me the street that it sits on was also the home of much black market activity after the war. "I used to take the number six," he repeats to himself, trying to remember the small details that once facilitated his daily commute. My eyes watch his eyes reach back in time. It is mesmerizing.

Bennet tells me that he also takes a patternmaking course for several months, through the ORT program, while he is in Munich. "I learned how to draw and size patterns for women's clothing. I loved it, because once clothes were made, I could see the results of my handiwork," he says. He seems genuinely fond of this era, this growth in himself, his learning. It will all bear fruit soon enough, although not entirely as he initially expects.

What does forgiveness look like? I wonder. I do believe, in part at least, it looks like just such scenes as these. I do believe I am catching the faint tinkling sound of musical notes around Bennet's head, as if it is his halo.

Yes, I do believe.

# CHAPTER 16

This morning it is sunny. Again: the couches, the face-off of our two worlds, his and mine.

"I used to love to dream I'm flying," he says, laughing.

"When have you dreamt that?" I ask.

"Mostly when I was a child but also when I got older sometimes." He gets excited and adds "I had a funny dream last night."

"Oh?"

"Yes, I dreamt something about a Mafia man in our building management business. He was chasing me or something. I couldn't understand why he was there or what he wanted. Ever since I was liberated from the camps, I dreamt about being chased, being caught and held down, and not being able to get out of something," he tells me more soberly. "Then I would wake up."

"I, too, remember dreaming of being held down but have no past reasons such as yours to be percolating that image," I tell him. "It is interesting, too, that I used to dream of flying. I have always felt like I flew before being here," I say "What do you mean 'here?'" he asks me.

Oh, dear. "Here on Earth," I say, wincing.

Bennet scoffs at this idea but not about the feeling of flying itself. I wonder: is the image of flying a symbol for being free, unfettered? Maybe it has more meaning but such ideas sometimes get in the way of what someone else has to say, so I leave it to float in the air between us.

Curiously, he offers, "I trained myself to forget my bad dreams."

"What do you mean you trained yourself to forget them?"

"I would give myself a command to forget bad dreams right after I woke up."

"Did you have these dreams often?" After anyone has suffered traumatic experiences or violence, it is common to dream, re-process what has happened, either re-living the past, or creating in the dream an outcome different from the actual experience lived.

"Oh, sure," he says expecting this question. "For maybe twenty years, maybe more, I used to have bad dreams a lot. When I would be sleeping with someone, sometimes I'd kick them in my sleep, trying to get away. One time I even got up and kicked the wall in my sleep and didn't remember doing it."

"So you trained yourself to just forget them?" I ask, again incredulous.

"Yes," he repeats. "I'm really happy now when I wake up," he adds.

So Bennet does think about how he thinks.

"It is amazing how the human mind works, don't you think?" I ask him.

"Yes, can you imagine?" And he laughs.

And I know that one of the aspects about Bennet that is intriguing to me is not just the fact that he survived the war. I have told him many times, "You are more than three and a half years in the camps." Sometimes it seems to be a small part of his life, in retrospect. Certainly in time that is true. But what is equally intriguing is that he discovers creative ways to transcend so much of that horror, even if not all of it can be eliminated. Amazingly, I see him marvel at his own efforts, turning the dark into light as best he can, whether he words it this way or not inside his own mind.

And yes, he has another talent.

Bennet also writes out not just what he has witnessed from his brutal years. He also reveals the stretch of a cat, reaching to unburden what haunts him in a poem he wrote some years after. The stretch is not just to pass the haunting. It is for something far greater, too.

Bennet stretches for love. He stretches for it because he knows it is there, somewhere. It is not beyond his vision.

Awaken from slumber, from treacherous nights
Of pain and misery
Nights filled with haunted voices
Trying to run away from memories of the past,
Turned and twisted.
Stretching to find a cool place
To revitalize bones
That walked their soles down to raw blisters
Over the stench of feelingless bodies
That once cried for help
Oh, where are the floating rivers
That kiss the shores
And rocks that stick out
Wanting to be wetted with its juices
That burst the bulbs to bloom
The seedlings to grow,
The thin grasses so soft.
I hear the roaring of its forces
Trying to reach calmer shores
To run smoothly to the river delta.
How can I make the world
Turn that fast on its axis?
How can I fill the days, weeks and months,
That are rushing by?
I want the earth to stop
So I can fill it with love,
For its millennium of revolutions.
I am but a speck or grain
That was washed from ocean to ocean
To reach a welcoming shore.

And now its frame filled with a sweet smell
Wants to kiss the beauty of creation.

II

Bursting tentacles searching for love,
Reaching out to touch and hold,
Velvet softness caressing its beauty
Hoping and wishing that its lasting will never be enough.

Shining sun through dark clouds,
Its rays piercing to the waiting meadows,
Nourish me with your life-giving light,
Its brightness and warmth will erase its shadows.

And when darkness comes and covers the earth,
Don't fill my heart with sadness,
Open my eyes to the portals of love
For it is then, in the quiet moments,
That two hearts become one.

■

# CHAPTER 17

In 1948 I became very ill. I had a high fever, a headache, and general pain all through my body. Luckily, a friend was visiting me, and I asked her to call my cousin Ludvig, who was a policeman in the DP camp. She found a phone (we had none in the apartment) and called him. Ludvig arrived, and both of them took me to the hospital. The doctors tapped my spinal fluid, and diagnosed the disease as meningismus, an inflammation of the tissue covering the neck and brain, resulting in severe headaches and sensitivity to light. I was treated well by a Polish nurse. After doses of penicillin and other medications, my spinal fluid appeared to be normal, and I was discharged after two weeks.

I continued my studies at the music school. On the Christian holiday celebrating Jesus' ascent to heaven, I was chosen to sing two songs at the cathedral; one of the songs was Beethoven's "Die Himmel Ruhmen" (The Skies Are Lauding). Afterwards, the rector of the church wrote me a beautiful letter, saying that he was touched, considering that I was Jewish.

In addition to my voice teacher at the academy, I studied with a private teacher named Elsa Domberger, who was from a well-known family in Germany. She was so wonderful that she didn't care that I could not always pay for my lessons. I would eat at her home quite often. Her father was a famous portrait artist, and her mother was confined to a wheelchair. One day she invited Georg Solti (now a Sir), the great conductor who was then the director of the symphony, to listen to me sing a few arias. She was hoping that the Bavarian Culture Ministry would give me a stipend to pay for my rent and lessons. I spoke with him in Hungarian, and indeed he arranged a scholarship for me.

Oh, my, this is no small skill Bennet reveals to Maestro Solti. Georg Solti even then was quickly becoming a world-class musical director and conductor. Georg Solti was born in Budapest as Gyorgy Stern. His father changed his name to avoid anti-Semitism, moving the family to Switzerland during the war to avoid persecution. After the war, Solti became music director of the Bavarian State Orchestra in Munich and the Frankfurt Opera. Further, he later became the conductor of The Los Angeles Philharmonic, the Chicago Symphony Orchestra and the London Philharmonic Orchestra.

Bennet sang for this man. Solti heard the voice and arranged for a scholarship. Bennet is breathing music. Bennet is not living a nightmare. Bennet is living a wonderful dream and in it, he is making his own garden, forever breathing life into it. Bennet is growing new life in abundance, like shoots off a plant.

Once, when he was in Munich he wanted to go to a sold-out concert but no tickets were available. The concert was a performance by violinist Yehudi Menuhin, someone he admired very much. He tells me he hung around outside the concert hall, hoping against hope for some great good fortune to come his way, for one of his famous pieces of luck.

"I asked all kinds of people if they had any tickets to sell. They all said 'no,'" he says with firmness. "Then I found two U.S. servicewomen and asked them," he continues. "They said they had an extra ticket and they invited me to go with them. They even made arrangements for me to have tickets for other concerts that I could pick up and attend without them" he tells me, excitedly.

Amazing.

"Can you imagine? When I was little we didn't even have a radio in our house in Zdenevo. But my dad loved music and played the violin. I admire genius—in music and in science," he tells me.

I am so captivated, so affected by Bennet's energy, his enthusiasm. Is this what happened to the servicewomen?

"Who are your favorite composers?" I wonder aloud.

"Beethoven, Mozart, Bernstein," he pauses, "I can't remember my favorite American composer, it starts with a C. I must be getting old," he laughs, hunching his shoulders, part abandon and giggle.

Then, abruptly: "Copeland—he's my favorite American composer." He sighs with satisfaction. I cannot tell if the satisfaction comes from remembering the name or the sweet memory of the man's music. No matter; the effect is the same, for the whole category is one that fills him up, feeding a hidden spot inside.

> In 1949, I received my visa to travel to America. Elsa Domberger begged me not to go, pleading with me that she had plans for my future in the Munich Opera. However, I was too young to listen to her good ideas, and felt that I could accomplish more in the United States. Little was I to know that many years later, in 1972, I would be in Europe with my children, attending my niece Rutica's wedding. Rutica's father, Miklosh, was my brother-in-law, married to my sister Cilly. He took Len and me by car to Yugoslavia. When we stopped in Munich overnight, I looked up Miss Domberger in the telephone book. Sure enough, she was listed, and I called her. She was in her eighties by then, and when I told her, "This is Bence" (my German name), she could hardly believe it. I bought some flowers and went over to her house. What a touching experience: I cried, she cried, and so did Len. We reminisced for an hour about how wonderfully I had been treated in her house. We said good-by with tears in our eyes.

Oh dear, oh dear.

> In the beginning of June, 1949, I went by train to Bremen, where I boarded an American Navy ship. The ship was full of refugees who elected me to write a daily newspaper, since I spoke all their languages. But as soon as the ship left port, I got seasick. I was given a cabin with a typewriter, but could not spend even an hour at the desk. I was so sick that I could not eat, and spent the whole time lying down.
>
> I left many good friends behind in Germany. I had spent many weekends in Wasserburg, seeing friends who had come from Poliana and other parts of

the Carpathians. I had met a girl from Svalyava, whose name was Anicka. She was petite and very beautiful. She had come once to Munich and had stayed in my room. There had been no way for her to get home that same day. However, in those days a man did not sleep with his girlfriend before they got married, so I let her stay in my bed, while I went down the block to sleep at a little inn. We really liked each other. In 1948, she left for the States, and we would write to each other (I still have the letters she wrote). Sometimes she would slip five dollars into her letter. I was sure that I would marry her one day.

"How could you leave," I ask Bennet, "with such promise in your musical future?"

"I always wanted to go to America, always. I thought I could sing there, too," he says simply.

The pull for America is so strong. We natural-born citizens hear this but take it for granted. It is not our "fire in the belly." It is the immigrants, born somewhere else, that truly know it, feeling its flames.

It still burns in Bennet. It's in the eyes.

But of course there is something else that beckons.

Someone, actually.

Kalvin.

The same blood pours through both their veins. Between Kalvin and America, Munich never really did stand a chance.

America is a vast conspiracy
to make you happy.

*— John Updike*

# CHAPTER 18



"How long did you live like this? How long had Kalvin been here at this point? What had he been doing to earn a living? Were other family members planning on coming? Was there a plan?"

My questions come fast and furious, the intrigue great. After all, Bennet has migrated from a difficult but nevertheless, in ways, euphoric several years in Germany.

Now in New York, in a sea of Americans, there is Kalvin. Though there is also a Martin, there is principally Kalvin. While the potential for a future life looms large, it is not without complications. The commingling of surviving freedom in a new country and gazing back on the horror and sorrow one has recently left, presents confusion in uncharted territory.

"Martin Greenfield lived with his family in Pavlovo, fifteen or twenty miles from our village of Zdenevo. We met after the war—Kalvin met him—in Wasserburg, in the DP camp. Martin had cousins from the same village as ours, so it was common to come across people you knew from your area," he says matter-of-factly.

"It was common?"

It was common to just bump into one another in another country five hundred miles from their original home and then again five thousand miles away, once in New York? How does this happen if not for providence? How does this happen if not for destiny? Is it really the same as the rock falling from the cliff—that serendipitous?

After a slight pause, Bennet continues. "Martin had cousins in the U.S. so he came first. It was easier to come if you had relations here."

"And Kalvin? How did he beat you here?" I ask.

"He was a minor and it was easier to get sponsored if you were under age—a child," he tells me. "It took me three years to get my visa."

"How did you like New York and the U.S. when you first came?" I ask next.

"I loved the freedom. I was impressed that people could stand out on a corner and criticize anything, the government, anything, and not get arrested. The left wingers used to stand on Fourteenth Street and criticize the U.S. and talk up Russia. It made me mad what they said but I was amazed that they could say it."

"And what do you think about it now?" I ask.

"Then, I thought people didn't understand where other people stood in the world, that they couldn't say these things without a bad result. I think that's even true now but maybe not as much as then," he tells me.

"I loved what America had to offer. During the Korean War I gave blood and went so far as to talk to an army recruiter—to maybe volunteer," he tells me looking amazed. "Sometimes I think I'm a bigger patriot than people born here," he says, laughing, almost shyly. I am inclined to believe him.

"I knew even then there is no place like America, knew I was blessed for being able to come here. Where else can you do what you want?" he challenges me, pushing the air into my space. "When you don't have freedom, it can be very bad."

And Bennet would certainly know.

So much we take for granted being cradle Americans, even the poorest of us still born into political privilege.

"When the recruiter found out I knew all these languages he was very interested in me. He told me I could do intelligence work, that they would drop me behind enemy lines in Czechoslovakia. I told him 'no, no, no' because I had already been through hell over there," Bennet says.

"Did you ever regret leaving Munich? It sounds like everything here was such a struggle initially, and leaving the music must have been so very hard. Was it?"

There is a noticeable shift in his posture—stiffness—a kind of clarity surrounds Bennet on the couch, one you can almost touch, collected into the form of the man himself, pressing in on him like gravity.

"When I first came I wasn't very happy; I wanted to go back to Munich. I had no job, no study, no income, and was living with my brother in a tiny place," he says, soberly.

"I realized I had made a mistake by coming to the U.S. so soon. But it was too late. I realized I should have stayed in Munich, made a name for myself in music, but I couldn't wait," he continues.

"And Kalvin was here," he says clear-eyed. It is the clear-eyed quality I have come to read as acceptance, pure and simple.

It is impossible for me to imagine the transition from opera singer on a path to becoming a professional singer, regarded by others as having great potential, to impoverished newcomer selling one's blood with the winos to get money for food. It is a lot to watch so much fade away as he is drawn to the siren song of America and, of course, always to Kalvin.

But if I have come to identify anything about Bennet, it is the instinct from which he functions—acceptance coupled with a quiet but fierce instinct to carry on without complaint. It has not only saved his life innumerable times, but it has advanced it for the better repeatedly. He seems to operate from an uncanny faith.

"So it was mixed, your view of coming here, yes?" I coax.

"Yes, I suppose it was," he offers, seeming a bit surprised at himself. "I wanted to come, I loved what the U.S. had to offer but I left some dreams behind."

The eyes go down, shaded, but I swear, he does not look sorry.

One day Anicka's brother came to discuss the situation between us. He told me how sad his sister was. Of course she could not wait a few years, because she was at the age when girls got married then. Though I did not marry for several more years, she soon married a young engineer with a good job, who had gone to school with me in Mukachevo. He had wanted to marry her forever, but she had liked me too much. They later had three children and lived in Munster, a suburb of Chicago.

Around 1991, I was told that her husband had died, so I wrote her a condolence note and gave her my telephone number. Eventually, she invited me to visit her. I told her that when I visited my son in Madison, Wisconsin, I would pay her a visit. A few months later, after visiting Leonard and his family, I took a bus from the Chicago airport to see her. She was waiting for me in her car at the bus station. I recognized her, we hugged, and I joined her for lunch at her home, where we talked endlessly about old times, and about what we had been through over the forty-two years in which we had not seen each other. But she was no longer like the picture I had had in my head; she was not the same petite girl that I remembered. I know that I have changed, too, but more than anything, we had established different lifestyles. I enjoy music, the theater, and traveling. She took care of some property that she owned, but never went to the theater, and did not participate in the world I lived in. I saw right away that we had grown in different directions.

Anicka invited me to stay the night, but I did not want her to have the wrong impression, so I said that I had to leave that afternoon. To make a long story short, she came to Los Angeles for a visit and wanted to stay at my house. I told her that this would not look right, so she stayed at her cousin's home. After she left, she wrote me a letter suggesting that we get serious, but I replied that I did not wish to marry again. In response, she sent me back the sweater and perfume that I had given her while she had visited Los Angeles, and that was the end of our story.

Lost loves—some are recoverable in the right time or circumstance; some are not. When it becomes obvious, as it has in Bennet's mind, that each has grown in very different directions, a chapter in a life often ends. That lost love takes on a larger context, a different scrutiny because you see yourself anew; not just where you've come from, the distance you've traveled, but where you are now. It is the kind of view that definitely cements you in the present.

So I ask him, "Why did you contact her?"

"Well, I suppose I was curious. I had been in love with her," he whispers.

"I suppose it's natural," I tell him, "to want to know if there is any spark that could be rekindled.

"But it sounds like you had become different people, not just from each other but from what you each were from yourselves when you were younger, yes?"

"I guess that's true," he affirms, a bit reluctantly.

He can't help but repeat as if it still surprises him, "I just don't feel we had anything in common. She hadn't traveled much and that was important to me. Plus, I got the feeling she wasn't very close to her children and I didn't like that," he finishes, lifting his chin.

Yes. Family.

While eating lunch a bit later, from my side of the table I ask him quietly, "If there's anything you could change from this aspect of your past, what would it be?"

"Marry Anicka," he says swiftly. Surprisingly, it is an unequivocal response. "Back in the early days."

"Wow," I breathe.

He looks up from his soup bowl, then rises, fidgeting around the kitchen. "I had been through an unhappy marriage. Maybe if I had married Anicka, it would have been different, better."

"But you said you didn't have anything in common," I remind him.

"Yes but maybe we could have grown in the same way if we had married when we were young. It could have been different."

I think back to Bennet's poem and to his elaboration of this love story played out so differently in the early days in New York. The steam engine that is duty of a different sort plows fast and furious. He did not feel prepared to take a wife yet a part of his heart had been hers.

Duty, responsibility, bond of family, freedom and opportunity, Kalvin.

Anicka, Munich, opera.

I know Bennet loves numbers but how would he ever have been able to calculate the potential gains and losses, the costs and benefits of the choices he ultimately settles on at this time. It is 1949; 1950 is on the horizon. His life will be re-directed soon enough. Yes, there is to be an entirely new Mermelstein ecosystem morphing into the promise that is America. It includes its own music, its own people, and its own opportunity.

■

# CHAPTER 19

"**S**o how did you manage things? How long did it take you to adjust to life in America?"

"It took a few months but soon I got a job. I worked in a tea and coffee packing plant. Later I worked in a zipper factory. The hours at the zipper factory were difficult, from six p.m. to two a.m. I would be so tired I'd fall asleep on the subway back to Brooklyn. My stop was Flatbush but I'd often sleep past it, all the way to Sheepshead Bay."

"I also began to sing, to be hired for bar mitzvahs and that kind of business," he tells me. "One singing job for a friend and word got around and spread quickly."

I also sang for various organizations. When I sang one performance for B'nai B'rith, at a temple, a gentleman approached me and asked if I would consider working that summer as a bellhop in the mountains. I was excited to do this, and in July I went by bus to Woodbridge, to the Hotel Glory. I was quite popular at the hotel, and became friendly with Mrs. Levy, a beautiful, fine person who was the wife of one of the partners.

After we spoke a few times, she asked me why I, who spoke so many languages and seemed so educated, was working in my capacity. I told her that I had just come from Germany and needed to earn some money.

One Saturday evening, the scheduled entertainer failed to show up. I went up to the director, an elderly woman, and told her that if necessary, I could sing a few songs. She looked at me, and condescendingly replied, "What do you think this is, a joke?" I told her that I was serious, that I had studied singing and could perform in five languages. I assured her that I would not make a fool of myself. She talked it over with the boss, and he agreed that if the entertainer did not show up within fifteen minutes, I could sing.

In the meantime, I walked over to the musicians and asked them if they knew any Italian songs. The pianist told me his repertoire of popular songs, and we chose a key for me to sing in. A few minutes later, the director pushed over and said, "Fast, fast, let's go." She introduced me as "Bennet the bellhop." I came on stage and announced that I would sing a few Italian and Jewish songs, with the help of the pianist. After I completed my first song, the whole audience stood up and clapped. When I was finished, they did not want me to go off stage. From that point on during entertainment nights, the people would clap and shout, "We want Bennet," over and over. The director was not so happy that I would leave what I was doing to go on stage to sing a few songs.

I became the most famous bellhop in the Catskills. I worked for six weeks, and left with $625—a lot of money in 1949. I had been appreciated and well liked by the guests and by the young people. I had worked hard at many things—giving water to the card players, administering permanents to the ladies (the kind that came prepared in a package), and singing when needed. I met many people with whom I stayed in touch after I returned to New York City, and I stayed in touch with the Levy family so that I could know how Mrs. Levy was feeling, since she had become ill. I learned that it takes no more effort to be nice and helpful than it does to be nasty and bad. This has been my motto throughout my life, a lesson that I still preach to my children all the time.

I am looking around Bennet's study. He has pictures of himself singing into a microphone, a picture of Barbara Streisand in New York when she was younger, autographed to him, other pictures of him performing. In addition, Bennet has shown me numerous playbills of programs he was in or directed over the years, all confirming a man meant to sing, something—anything.

I know why the caged bird sings. Of course!

I returned to Brooklyn, where we rented a room at Mrs. Feingold's apartment at 1585 East 14th Street. A widow in her seventies, she treated us as if we were her own children. Eventually Steve also came to the United States, and he shared that single room with Kalvin, Martin, and me. Mrs. Feingold liked me—she would call me "Bengyi." I'd help her with her shopping, have discussions with her, and read the mail to her. The other boys joked that she would leave me money in her will because I was so kind to her. I didn't receive an inheritance from her, but a few years later, her daughter called me to tell me that she had passed on, and that it had been her wish before she died that I chant the prayers at her funeral. After the funeral, her children told me how their mother had always mentioned me. They thanked me and we said 'good-bye.'

I soon got a job singing in the choir at the Eastern Parkway Synagogue, where Hershkovitz was the cantor. This job paid me nicely. I found other opportunities to sing quite easily. I even sang at a luncheon at the Carnegie Building, where Mrs. Roosevelt was a guest. I sat next to a Dr. Zouchelly. After I had sung a few songs, he told me that I had a beautiful voice. He said he had heard that I had not been in New York for a long time, and he asked how I liked the United States. I told him how I loved it, but complained that I was waking up each day with terrible headaches. Dr. Zouchelly took out his card and told me to contact him the next time I had a headache. I learned that he was Mrs. Roosevelt's and Mayor La Guardia's doctor.

The following Monday morning, sure enough, I woke up with my headache. I called the doctor's office, and the secretary replied, "OK, the doctor can see you in about three months." I said, "No, the doctor told me to call him and that he would see me right away. Please tell him that I am the singer who sang for Mrs. Roosevelt, and that I would like to see him today." She said, "Just a minute." After a few moments, the doctor himself got on the phone, and told me to go to a certain office, where I would get a head and spinal x-ray. He also told me not to pay for the x-ray, but to bring it right to him at his office somewhere near Park Avenue.

I did as he told me, and showed up at his office later that day. He was a chiropractor as well as a physician—but I had no idea about what a chiropractor was since I was so new in the country. After he had looked at the x-ray he called me in, examined me, and took a history about my injuries. I went into another room where I lay down on a special cot while he manipulated my spine and neck. I was scared that he was going to break my bones, but he calmed me down and told me just to relax. Afterwards, he took me into another room, where the lighting was very dim, and he told me to close my eyes and sleep. I slept for about twenty minutes, and when I woke up my headache was gone. I could not believe this. The doctor came in, and I kissed his magical hands. He was glad that I felt better, and told me that if the headaches returned, I should just call the office and come over again.

I got dressed and asked the secretary how much I owed the doctor. She told me that the doctor did not want me to pay anything, and she reiterated that I should call again if the headaches returned. Sure enough, after a few weeks I was experiencing headaches again. I called the doctor, and received the same treatment. Altogether I visited him three times, and to this day I seldom have headaches. When I told him that I did not feel right about not paying, he said, "Someday you'll be a famous singer, and then you'll pay." Several years later when I was doing better financially, I brought him a dozen bottles of champagne at Christmas, to express my gratitude for his earlier help.

How does one value kindness? And how does it come into someone's life unbidden? Bennet is wedged between two worlds: to extend kindness, and to receive it back. In essence it is the same world with one half of the globe taking in and the other blowing out—one single act filled to capacity from opposite sides of the bellows. He has told me that when you are good to people it comes back to you in some way, at some time.

I must rest his case.

A bit later I asked him to go back and tell me about Rochester, when he first came to the U.S. "And family, what was everyone doing in the first few years after you came to America?" I asked.

"When I first came I went to Rochester, New York, to audition for the Eastman School of Music. They accepted me but I could not attend because I had no money," he says flatly.

"But you said they would give you a scholarship."

"Yes, but I had nowhere to stay, no money for living expenses. Kalvin was in New York. I couldn't leave Kalvin."

Silence. And then a small ache.

Are the pictures on Bennet's walls paying attention to this? Do the plants in the room feel the commitment of two brothers? Are they bending in Bennet's direction, as if to sunlight? Is the energy of the one brother supporting the energy of the other, each together? One familial ecosystem indivisible under an American sky; they have transported their photosynthesis across the Atlantic. It is a Mermelstein frame built on a Jewish foundation that remains inseparable to this day, regardless of who is living and who has passed on. I see it in Bennet, his brother Steve, hear it when Bennet has called sister Cilly in Israel, and it is to trickle down in all their children who, while unborn in 1949, will show their next-generation faces soon enough.

"So what about the rest of your brothers and sisters from Europe; was there a plan for everyone to come?"

"No plan but everyone wanted to come at some point, if they could," he tells me. "Of course they wanted to come," he repeats.

"Yes," I acknowledge.

"Steve comes next after a few years in London; then Shary, Esty from Hungary, later Cilly and her husband from Budapest." The three in Israel stay in Israel.

"And you all find ways to work?"

"Yes. Kalvin works at the Three G's clothing factory with Martin. When Steve comes, he will get a job in Buffalo."

"So you all just go about the business of building new lives."

"Yes," he confirms. "You just do it."

"It must have been so hard, after all you had lost, all you had been through. It is incredible," I say, pointing my gaze into his face, firmly, insistently.

"It was nothing special, nothing extraordinary," he tells me, blowing out a little air. His response would make me laugh if I didn't recognize what an extraordinary thing it really had to have been, the true hardness of it all, trying to build a life from nothing in a new country, a new continent. No money. There is a pilgrim quality about immigrants coming to America and I witness a voyager with as much grit as I imagine those who landed at Plymouth must have displayed, so long ago. You really have to want it. And you have to be willing to work like hell.

Nothing special? Yes, it is, dear Bennet, yes, it is.

"Did you find a lot of newly transported European Jews when you came here?"

"Yes, and I, we, spent time with them, but also began to make friends with more and more Americans," he says, adding, "I liked Americans but felt they didn't know a lot of worldly things, they didn't know other foreign languages. This seemed strange to me."

"Sometimes I think Americans are naïve, or sheltered," I tell him. "We have had an easier life compared to those in many other parts of the world."

"Well, I don't exactly think they're naïve; they just don't have the same exposure or experiences and didn't during World War II, either," he says.

And then there's the inevitable truth about hard work.

Bennet is about to go into overdrive when it comes to work. Bennet knows full well how to activate a certain amount of ingenuity in order to thrive. It is a muscle he continues to exercise and develop, right along with the fierce intention that is in his DNA.

Always, the energy and determination; it's as if he is his own source. The double helix, electrified.

■

# CHAPTER 20

I also sang in a Jewish choir, where I was paid for both the rehearsals and the performances. The conductor was a Dr. Kopf, a German Jew. One day, he asked me to remain behind after the rehearsal. He asked why I was singing in his choir, and I told him that I had to make a living. He told me that he taught at Hebrew Union College, and suggested that I study for the cantorate. I replied that it was not my dream to be a cantor but to be an opera singer. He told me that this would be very difficult because I didn't have a sponsor and I had no money. He convinced me to audition for the cantorial school, so the next day I went to Sixty-Sixth Street, near Central Park, to audition. Since I had sung for many years as a choirboy, I knew most of the prayers. The people who listened to me were impressed, especially because I spoke Hebrew. They gave me a three-year scholarship to cover the duration of the program.

In between, I worked at the zipper factory. Cantorial school was easy—it was a Reform organization, and my years in Cheder had made me well versed in Hebrew liturgy and in the chants for each holiday. In February 1950, I was asked to audition for a cantorial and Hebrew-teaching job at the Flushing Jewish center, on Northern Boulevard and 171st Street in Queens. I didn't feel ready enough but went to the meeting anyway. It was Purim (a Jewish Holiday), and I was asked to sing some songs for that holiday. I did and also sang the aria from Tosca. The synagogue was searching for its first cantor. They enjoyed my performance, and hired me for $2,000 a year. Considering I was still attending school, this was an excellent salary. Back at the Academy of Music in Munich, I had been interested in designing women's clothes. I had always been good at drawing in school—my artwork had often been displayed on the walls. I had discovered an ORT school in Munich (an organization that teaches young people professions) where I had taken some lessons in patternmaking and design. Now in New York, I took a two-week refresher course at the CHICK Institute. Next, I found a job at Slender Styles on Broadway, where I was an assistant patternmaker. At the same time, I was preparing the Flushing Jewish Center boys for bar mitzvah, was teaching Hebrew and singing, running a children's and an adult choir. I conducted services every Friday evening, Saturday morning, and Saturday afternoon. On Sunday mornings, we would have breakfast and I would conduct the prayers.

The amount of activity and work Bennet describes is staggering. "When did you sleep?" I ask.

He ignores me.

Instead, he has pulled out an old program from the box loaded with programs: things he conducted, items from the Jewish Center, thank you notes, bar mitzvah memorabilia.

"I can't believe I did it all," he says, shaking his own head in disbelief. "Then, I just did it, and worked six and a half days a week," he adds.

And then, a turning.

"You have told me you don't believe in God. How could you do this job? How could you be a cantor? It seems a conflict," I say, perplexed. "When did you stop believing in God?"

"It started in the camps and after liberation. Also, during the Iran—Iraq war both sides claimed 'Allah will save us; Allah will make us victorious.' Silly," he says, but then ratchets it up. "It was ridiculous."

He seems angry, his arms tightening across his chest, digging in.

"But being a cantor—the singer of prayers?" I press.

The temperature rises in the room as he squeezes his arms tighter, lips pursed.

Then, something quite amazing happens. All of a sudden Bennet is relaxed, at peace, even. His face is smooth, revealing sparkling, happy eyes. It is a marvel, really, and I sense time has slowed as if making room for his coming description.

"It's like a play when you are in a part, or an opera. You know, you become that character. I was a representative of the people, and felt a part of them. Plus, I knew what the prayers meant. Some of them are so beautiful; they used to move me to tears. I could feel the people, feel the connection with them. I could do it because they believed and I felt connected to them," he tells me.

He appears to have thought this through and it assumes a sort of logic. I picture an extension ladder with Bennet climbing skyward and all of them holding the base of it. So naturally, he plays a unique role in one combined effort of Jewish integration.

He continues. "I put myself in the spirit of honesty, of their belief. I put myself into that mode, that mental state—like a zone. I even fasted like they did before I would sing the prayers."

And there it is. A small catch in my throat occurs as I see without any doubt that prayer and an understanding of something greater than self can be expressed differently for each of us, and has no greater or lesser power or effect. The Chinese say "the way of the bird is not the way of the fish." I know this to be true from my own life as well as from watching Bennet's. For I have come to know that both belief in a higher order of things and an effort to communicate with it occurs at the level of our own experience.

More recently, Bennet has shown me the temple in Venice, California, where he was a cantor for years. I understand there were times on Friday nights when he was so exhausted from work that the last thing his physical body and mind wanted to do was go sing for services. Yet, he went. He sang. He prayed for them. I also asked Bennet once what he thought about the concept of sacrifice. He looked at me quite perplexed and then said, "I don't believe it. What you do is a gift or it is nothing."

And of course, this is what I witness in Bennet. He gives without expecting anything in return. Giving does not deplete him. Rather, it completes him.

He continues making his way in the world, an ongoing life force with substance and commitment, tender and sensitive to be sure; to that intangible quality some might call soul. It no longer seems terribly relevant whether he believes in an Old Testament God or not. He has operated from a higher-order energy system just the same. He cannot convince me otherwise.

He goes back to a familiar theme. "People in the camps died asking for God's help. Where was he? There was no God to save them." Pain and frustration reddens his face. "My best friend still died."

"But you didn't," I counter, flinching.

There is a hard stare coming from Bennet's direction, and while I feel his pain, I cannot know its depths.

This echoes throughout the room in which we tangle, as if the event were yesterday. He carries this tragedy still, holding it close so many, many years after the fact. The magnitude of death he saw was so massive he had nowhere else to go in his thought system but to excommunicate God. How arrogant of me to proscribe what his conclusions ought to be.

But here's the thing. They say Columbus was disappointed in his search for the Indies—but in its place he discovered a new world. This is so much how I view Bennet these days—his apparent loss of a country, a continent, opera, a tribe as well as a family, at least in the way he has known it, places him instead in New York—a new world to be sure, in which to receive for the whole man that which he could not give himself in Munich, by any of the individual splintered parts of his life.

Instead, it feels inescapable that cantoring was to do this for him. That what he was to receive from it would address him entirely, reorienting him and creating wholeness where splintering previously existed. He may not have gotten the answers he wanted to prayers he leveled in God's direction from the camps, angry and shouting at the soil or wailing in the wind. But Bennet received something greater because cantoring reunited him with life and with those who ask of him to join them, struggling as they might against the discords of daily living, through the music of prayers drifting forever higher.

In no time at all Bennet jumps and says, "Want a bite?" and he is off in a flash. It has become the signal to end the session. He yells from the kitchen, "Would you like some soup?"

"Yes," I say, but I sit in a moment of contemplation. Some say that communion with nature, enjoyment of art, poetry, or music is an expression of the divine, that an act of kindness may be a prayer for some, that work is an affirmation of that same creative power, that the living of a man can be a prayer in and of itself.

"You do want soup? Or you don't?" he calls.

"I would love some," I say, more loudly. I sigh and smile, rising in surrender to the inevitable routine of Bennet's household, enjoying the simple expression of eating as a shared activity. In a way, our time together also feels like a ladder, each of us taking turns holding the base or rising to the top of it, reaching for the sense of continuity, ultimately struggling to see both the blessing and the wholeness of an individual life, a view that only distance can afford.

It is a gift or it is nothing.

# CHAPTER 21

I soon met a beautiful girl, Carole, the daughter of the president of the temple. Her mother introduced her to me at a temple dance. We courted for six months. By then, I was in my late twenties and I thought it was time to settle down and raise a family. In 1952, we got married at the Flushing Jewish Center. We had a large wedding, and did not have much money for our honeymoon. Carole's aunt gave us a coupon for a hotel in Atlantic City, where we spent a week.

Carole worked at an office in New York; I was still attending school and working as a cantor and at various other jobs. I also sang in the Amato Opera Theater, where I had the roles of Don Giovanni and La Forza del Destino. But I could not pursue the opera as a profession in the way I had dreamed, because I needed too much money and time.

After six months, Carole quit her job. We were living on Chrocheron Avenue in an apartment. From the beginning, our marriage had problems. The relationship between Carole and her mother was very edgy, though her father was an extraordinary man. He was gentle and adored his wife tremendously—anything she did was good, in his eyes. But Carole was the eldest of three girls, and I think she was denied attention; this probably explained the strife between her mother and herself. I, in contrast, came from a family that was very close. Carole's mother was not on speaking terms with her own mother, who didn't even attend our wedding. She also didn't communicate with her own sister. I wanted to be close to my own family, but Carole did not let me.

> My married life did not proceed in the way that I had dreamed it would. We argued about everything. In 1953, our first child was born, and I was so happy that after having lived through the camps, I was able to have a child. We named her after my mother and my grandmother—in Hebrew, Chana Reisel; in English, Laura.
>
> I thought that a child would improve our marriage, but I was mistaken. For a few days peace would rule, but the pressure was always there. Carole complained that I didn't earn enough money or that I spent too much time outside the house. She developed a weight problem and could not keep to a diet. She loved cream cheese sandwiches and ice cream. I'd design a dress for her at the factory where I worked as a patternmaker, but by the time I would bring it home, it wouldn't fit. Going out on a Saturday night was a catastrophe—she would try on her dresses and I'd tighten her girdle, but it was all to no avail. And always, she would get so angry. She claimed it was my fault—I didn't make the dress the right size, or I took the measurements wrong—that sort of thing. The stress was so bad that even our sex life suffered.

This train seems to have gotten off the tracks so quickly, I think. "Why did you marry her?" I ask Bennet. "What qualities were you drawn to in her?"

"She was beautiful, like I said," he tells me. So he married the prettiest flower in the bunch.

"But what else? What was she like in the beginning?" I prod.

Bennet seems reticent, at a loss for words, and then says, "In the beginning she seemed nice, attentive. She would come with me to the Temple, waiting for me. We would talk and she seemed understanding in the beginning. This is what I saw. I dated her for about six months but later could see I hadn't really known her very well. I was naïve."

"What did Kalvin think?"

"Kalvin was married and living in New Jersey with Ruthy. He and Martin said 'maybe you should get married.' And her father seemed to like the match, too. It seemed the right time," he says simply, adding, "I was in love with her. I wouldn't have married her if I wasn't in love with her."

"And early on there was no evidence of problems with her family, and how she or they didn't always get along?"

"No, I didn't see it," he adds. "I respected her father a lot, and her mother seemed to like me in the beginning. Later on that changed, with her mother, though."

"But you say from the beginning there were problems. It must have been a mix—you must have had some good times, yes?" I poke.

"Well, yes, in the beginning there were some happy moments. We liked to go out on Saturday nights and sometimes we had lots of fun. There were two couples we would go with to movies, the theater. And Saturdays afternoons we would go to her parents' house."

"But within that early time there was also evidence of things not working well?"

"Yes, we used to fight; she was difficult, nothing was good enough, and I thought that unless she improved, I'd continue to have problems," he says. "I kept focused on other things—work at the temple six and a half days a week, always working hard. But it was very difficult. I did a lot in the house after coming home, changing diapers, taking care of the kids."

I notice Bennet sinking into his couch, arms tight across his chest, the tension rising all the while he is telling me about this growing unhappiness in his marriage. He has told me before he does not wish to focus in any great detail on this chapter of his life, respecting her legacy and her family's, and his own children's. Even so, he can't help but communicate something grown dark, though it is obvious he keeps details to himself. Fair enough. You keep your secrets, I'll keep mine.

While I have pulled out some small shards of light, some qualities about Carole, the mother of his children—her early attentiveness, her beauty, her apparent playful side—that he was undoubtedly drawn to in the beginning, it is clear it was a very thin foundation on which to build a life. The clearer side of their differences was not in evidence. Beauty hides many things, especially in the young. I, myself, know of which I speak.

"I was naïve." Probably so, but given where he's been, I'd imagine it would be hard to sort things out, to see people from a clearer perspective. Bennet once told me, "When you come here to America, after that time in the war, you don't think straight." Remarkably, my own flashback of marrying an incredibly handsome man crosses my mental screen. And I had nothing like his reasons. When you're young, it's easy to be drawn to the pretty in the world.

In 1956 we had a son, whom we named after Carole's father, Leo, who had passed away of an inherited heart condition when Laura was about seven months. We moved in with Marian, Carole's mother, for a while. I got along with my mother-in-law and Carole's sister, but she did not. Eventually, we moved to another apartment. In our first apartment, we had lived close to a man who was related to the secretary of my synagogue. He snored so loudly that we could hear him in our place.

We grew more and more unhappy. I was going through hell living in this marriage. Carole could not stand the situation, either. There was nothing more that I could do to make her happy. I was only glad we had a son and a daughter. They were both good children.

By 1960, my brother Kalvin was living in California, and my brother Steve was in Buffalo. Kalvin and Steve traveled to New York to visit our sisters Shary, Esty, and Cilly. We decided that if we were to be successful in America, we had to do something together. I had learned that my financial future was limited if I were to remain a cantor. The career of a cantor was also demanding each day and on weekends as well.

My brothers and I thought that the three of us could work together. We found ideal opportunities seemed to be in the needle trade, and New York seemed to have the best jobs in this field. However, we could not find the ideal situation. Kalvin suggested that we travel to Los Angeles on vacation, and that we look into possibilities there. He felt that it was easier to start a new business there than in New York.

We talked to our wives and decided to give it a try. In July 1961, Carole and I went to California. We stayed in a motel on La Cienega, and my brothers and I searched downtown for business opportunities.

Throughout this time Carole did not allow us to feel very comfortable. She always had something to complain about. She wanted to spend time sightseeing and even wanted to go to San Francisco. She just could not understand our focus was to find a business opportunity. She could not accept the fact that we had no money.

A friend whom we had known back in Usti—Albert Simon—suggested that we try the contracting business. He suggested this even though all three of us had worked in the needle trade. We decided instead to stick to our original plan and continued our search.

Kalvin had learned the needle trade in Zdenevo. He had worked for a few years at the Three Gs, a men's clothing manufacturer that our adopted cousin Martin Greenfield later purchased. Steve had gone to the Fashion Institute of New York and had studied in England and now was a production manager at an outfit in Buffalo. I had been a patternmaker for four years in New York.

We decided to make the move to Los Angeles, and that we would relocate as soon as we could give up our jobs. When I told the temple that I was moving to California, they were sad and they made a banquet dinner in my honor. My whole family was invited. I was given a nice plaque and presents. After a few weeks, we packed up the car and drove across the country to Los Angeles. The children, Laura and Leonard, stayed with Carole's mother while we settled in and found an apartment.

On our trip out West, we stopped at the Petrified Forest National Park, the Grand Canyon, and some other beautiful sites. It took us a week to get to L.A. In the meantime, Kalvin found a location for our business at 405 E. Pico Boulevard, on the fourth floor. He rented a few sewing machines, a buttonhole maker, a sew-on button machine, an overlock, a hemming machine, and a hand iron. Carole and I found a little house on Sherbourne Drive, between Olympic and Pico. Our rent was $180 per month. When our furniture arrived, we moved in. Our savings totaled about $2,000 at that point. Kalvin and his family lived just a few blocks away.

And so, a new beginning. Will there be sunshine poking out from the clouds? The three brothers are to build lives together on the West Coast, and in the process, Bennet may eke out some hope within his own household. He certainly is on the cusp of discovering a business life that will excite and invigorate him. And he will pour himself into it—they all will—working very hard, the only way they know how. I can just smell the success hovering off the ocean. It is salty with just a small amount of sting. It will be only a short while before it makes landfall. The vegetation is thick with the three brothers' potential, the pungent smell of early blossoms close to overwhelming them.

"It was Kalvin's idea," echoes Bennet.

Yes. Kalvin.

■

Business without profit is not business
any more than a pickle is candy.

*— Charles F. Abbott*

# CHAPTER 22

’ve seen his pictures, you know.

Kalvin’s.

I’m denied meeting him in person. You’ll see why, soon enough.

In the pictures there is fire in the eyes, an impish quality, part light, part dark, but certainly infused with the love of life. He is a handsome man. One gets the feeling that besides his flash, which is clearly visible in rings and clothes, he has an energy that is so affirming, filled with excitement for living—but there is a withholding going on as well. It’s in the shadows, covering something.

One thing is certain: he does not withhold love for his brothers—a generosity that will manifest itself in their collective efforts creating a synergy all its own. That is not to say there won’t be disagreements down the road. How easy it is to fight with the ones we love. It changes nothing about commitment.

And so now we had a place equipped with modern machines, but we couldn’t find clients. I would go to the manufacturing buildings, starting at the top floor and working my way down. I presented the “big spiel” to all of the potential clients. I told them that we were three brothers newly arrived from the East. I assured them that we knew our business well. But most of the contacts just told us to come back when we could provide them with some references.

After a few days, a gentleman finally responded positively to my request. He heard my story and said, “I’ll give you a try.” He supplied me with three hundred skirts, all cut in big bundles, and showed me how he wanted them to look. Excited, I put the packages in the trunk of my car, and hauled them over to our factory.

Now we had work, but we had no workers. I stood outside the Cooper Building (at that time it was a manufacturing building) and asked the women outside if they would like to work. Five of them agreed, and I drove them over to the factory in my car. Some of these workers stayed with us for eighteen years, until we sold the factory after Kalvin passed away. Steve and Kalvin sat down at the machines and started to sew the skirts. Steve had to show the workers how to set the zippers. A friend of ours recommended a foreperson by the name of Julia, who also remained with us for all those years. All of us worked round the clock to get those skirts out.

First we had to make a few samples. When we completed them, I brought them over to the client. He liked them. After we completed the lot, he gave us additional projects, and we were able to hire more people to work in the facto-ry. Soon we had to go in to the factory on weekends to do all the things that we couldn't get to during the week: oiling the machines, cleaning the floors and tools, arranging the cut work into bundles, making payroll, and printing up the work tickets. Everything we did was piecework—that means that every worker was paid for each operation. For example, the operators or pressers got paid for the individual job, and the amount was printed on a work ticket; each job had its name and number.

My brothers and I did not draw salaries. For about six months, we relied on Steve's earnings, for he still had to complete some work in Buffalo. Finally, he too arrived in L.A. for good. We were determined to be a success. Slowly we became known as the "three brothers," and the business began to thrive. Steve found us a client known as Miss Pat that put us on our feet—and that was a boon for us. The Miss Pat Company increased its orders and brought us a lot of business in the years to come. We started to make money. Our workspace got to be too small, so in 1963 we moved to the corner of Santee and 11th Street, where we occupied the entire second floor, which was about 5,000 to 6,000 square feet. In this area we owned a boiler, two machine presses, six hand-iron pressers, one button-hole and two button machines, an overlock, a sew-over-lock, and about fifty single-needle machines. We still wrote our own work tick-ets, which Steve would prepare at his house. We constantly worked very hard.

In the same year, we purchased a factory called Julie K, located on Los Angeles Street. Steve ran that company, while Kalvin and I worked at the factory on Santee Street. By 1966 we had accumulated enough money to buy a lot for another factory, on Griffin and 14th Street. Under the company name Mermel & Mermel, we decided to construct a 15,000- square-foot building—10,000 for us and 5,000 to rent out. We wanted to rent some of it out so that we could have some help in paying the mortgage should difficult times occur.

"The Three Brothers" are developing a vibrant, critical-mass enterprise in downtown Los Angeles in the early days of the garment district's development. Kalvin's business experience pays off. His early foray into several enterprises both in New Jersey and in Los Angeles paves the way for the three brothers' eventual success. Bennet acknowledges that Kalvin was the brains, the idea man behind so much of what they were to grow, with Steve developing clients and handling the financials, and Bennet, the ferocious finishing production man, critical to getting the product out the door and on the trucks for shipment.

"Tell me more about the parking lot, and the building you built at Maple and 11th Street. What was the impact on your business success?"

"Well, we started renting space to jobbers out of the Alley. This was Kalvin's idea too." This attribution is never far from Bennet's descriptions.

"What exactly is a jobber?"

"A jobber is a business that buys out a manufacturer's product overflow and then turns around and sells it to stores. The product overflow is usually discounted," he informs me. "It caught on fast and within a year the trucks came in and out of the Alley at an overwhelming pace. Everyone was doing it. We had been the first to build and once it got rolling, the rental price per square foot was the most expensive in the country. Even more than Rodeo Drive," Bennet says, not so matter-of-factly, a bit of pride shining on his face.

"Some people used to buy what's called a key—paying a premium to buy out someone else's lease so they could sell from that location. The Garment District, from Olympic to Pico, between Santee and Maple, became huge. There were hundreds of stores with real and copied brands. Lots of bargains," Bennet tells me.

This fascinates me—this "rags to riches" sort of story that Americans love—but I don't share my small bit of awe. Instead, I ask if the early days were exciting for him. At this notion, he cocks his head but ultimately acknowledges that "sure, it was," smiling as he speaks.

"Did the success of all of this shock you?" I ask. This apparently seems even sillier to him. He nearly snorts.

"It didn't shock us because we had worked very hard. We employed a hundred and twenty people in our factories and had started at the ground level. In the beginning we didn't have any money. We paid each other fifty dollars a week until we got going, but we had worked hard always," he finishes.

"How long was it before you become profitable?" I pose.

"A year maybe, then it began to grow."

I am inspired. "Can you show me what you made? Can you show me?" I ask him.

"Sure. We can meet downtown and I will show you," he says.

I wonder what it means to Bennet's inner world to make such a business. He does not seem to take their monumental success for granted. Nor does he overstate it.

If you build it they will come. If the "Three Brothers" work really hard on a brilliant set of ideas, they will succeed. One follows the other like grass growing after a good rain.

But of course they'd succeed, like so much spontaneous combustion.

■

# CHAPTER 23

Today Bennet is driving me by their buildings in the garment district of Los Angeles. This is a different world and I am stunned by the gritty energy of it all.

"Now we rent only retail spaces since the jobbers no longer remained profitable," he says.

Lots of little stalls stand jam-packed with everything from wedding dresses to hats, sports shoes to umbrellas. As I listen to a staccato of multiple languages, I try to picture a younger Bennet moving quickly through the alleys. Today, as we thread our way between the shops, a man quickly spots Bennet, bows, and begins speaking in Spanish, which I do not understand. After their brief conversation, the man departs and Bennet tells me that a number of years ago he had helped the man keep his Korean restaurant when it was in danger of being shut down by the health department. Bennet had gone to the city council to help prevent its closing and the man was grateful into perpetuity. I wonder how many other people I know would have expended this kind of effort. Soon we are in the car and Bennet is beginning his tour for me to see their buildings, both current and formerly owned. When he drives me by the first building they had, the factory, I notice that the front façade is laced with stones cemented vertically, a style more common in the 1960s. "You don't see that very often," he tells me.

"No," I confirm. After touring past seven, eight of their buildings, we head back to his office on Maple Street. Once parked, we walk up the back way, snaking through stairwells of the city filled with its smells—food wrappers and musk, old concrete and seasoned iron. These vibrant causeways of commerce pump goods and services like blood through veins, keeping the financial organism alive. The happy messy chaos that is alley business is pungent and productive, stimulating in its efforts to fuel consumers and the city alike. I focus sharply on the three brothers' accomplishment, helping to create this commercial foundation in the Los Angeles garment district so many years ago.

The smell of food in kiosks triggers my own hunger and once back in Bennet's office, his secretary asks us what we want for lunch. She lets us know that his brother, Steve, is on his way in to the office and has ordered a vegetarian sandwich. "Would you like one?" Henrietta asks. A "yes" from each of us follows her down the hall like the hungry echo that it is. She has been with the company for thirty years. She wears her loyalty and efficiency well.

Bennet looks on his computer to see what the stock market is doing. "Some up, some down," he tells me. "If I had known that we would be in this economic mess, I would have taken my money out of the market." In a flash, he calls his broker.

"What's happening?" he asks her.

I watch him scrutinize numbers as he goes back and forth between looking at his computer screen and listening to her, peppering an "I'm telling you" and "can you believe it?" throughout. "I like to gamble," he says, clearly enjoying himself.

Because I understand little to nothing about finances, my mind wanders for the shortest of seconds. My eye catches his Sudoku puzzle beside his desk blotter and I help myself to it while he continues talking to her. It is completely filled out.

Interrupting himself again, he says, eyes twinkling, "I did it this morning."

Bennet's mind operates in numbers. It is a metric muscle that propels so much success, I imagine. Some recognize that making money is the caloric intake the commercial animal needs, not just to survive, but also to thrive. It is a kind of talent and focus I am not wired for, yet I am fully conscious of its value and worth. We would all be so very lost without the elements of society that provide this function. Simply put, without commerce, fairly and aggressively implemented, America's engine does not run.

It is fun to watch Bennet take pleasure in this world, knowing full well the individual effort and sweat required to make this business happen. He is a man of many talents—singing, languages, numbers, organization, profits. And while he may not focus on profits for profits' sake, he understands clearly profits as fuel—the natural resource that keeps the organism going, ever-increasing, ever-expanding.

"She is a nice lady, my broker. I've had her for many years," he says suddenly, hanging up the phone.

"How do you define success?" I ask him.

"Money is very important—to not be dependent on children; to be self-sufficient," he answers thoughtfully now, quite serious.

"Yes," I say, "but that's not all, is it?"

I watch the gears shift. "To be loved by people, to be honored, to have a good reputation is worth more than money."

I have to wait for the rest of it because I have learned that he will tell me more if I am patient.

"To have a good name. Every Sabbath when mother said prayers and lit candles, I remember my mother always lit a candle and said a silent prayer that her children should be loved by others."

He still carries his mother. Once again he breathes her memory out of himself.

"Every Friday she would hide bread in her clothes and give it to poor people in the town," he tells me. "When she died, the rabbi had put on her epitaph that she always had an 'open hand to all.'"

I think back to the man we came upon in the alley earlier today. Bennet's mother has reached into the future, coming out through her son in an alley in America. I think she would be proud.

The mood shifts as we are interrupted by scurrying in the hall. Bennet gets up from his desk, making his way to the door. All of a sudden:

"This is my brother, Steve."

I turn to see a slight man with hair that is white, eyes peering out of glasses that rise above oxygen tubing connected to equal parts face and the tank that sits on the floor beside him. He looks nothing like Bennet. This is a shock, although I can't for the life of me say why. In my own family, most of my siblings look more different than alike although certainly there are features we share. With Steve and Bennet, their frames might be similar, the eyes may still have that clear, nearly haunted quality, but there the physical similarities seem to end.

"It's a pleasure," I say, offering my hand.

"Yes," he says, looking me straight in the face with intelligent eyes, taking my hand. Instantly, I am aware that depending on oxygen or not, he has no small amount of energy himself. His hand is firm. His eyes are quick, narrowing their focus. What is it with this Mermelstein family? They seem to have gotten well-above-average energy genes; not fair, not fair, I think to myself. And like Bennet, Steve has voltage that is palpable.

Moving across the hall, we sit down to lunch at a table. As we split the sandwiches in half, we seem to alternate between easy and awkward conversing. I can't help but be curious about Steve, in part because I have only known him through Bennet's telling.

"What is your background?" he asks of me.

"I've done marketing and public relations in the book business for many years. I also produced a program for Public Television, as well as live productions, including several programs with Steve Allen and one with Garrison Keillor, among others."

Steve asks me more about the work I do with Bennet, about his story, its length and scope. I tell him that it includes the camp years, the struggle. "But his life is so much more than the three and a half years in the camps, as you know, much more," I say.

Steve stares, seeming uncertain but then moves on. "I have a book a gentleman was helping me with," he tells me.

"Oh?" My curiosity rises.

"Yes, but he died. Even before he died, though, he stopped working on it. He had worked a lot with some Hollywood types, writing their stories, but moved to Colorado to raise dogs," he says, bluntly.

"Tell me some of your story. I understand you hid during the war. Where all did you hide?" I ask him.

"My sister hid me in the hospital, in Budapest."

"Did you hide other places?"

"Yes," he says, keeping the locations to himself.

"Did you use aliases?"

"No, but I used another name sometimes," he offers, hesitating.

I am confused because this seems the same as an alias to me but I don't press. While my instinct is to grill him, unearthing some of his life's details that I cannot help but be curious about, I remain quiet, waiting, waiting. Certainly there is more but it is not forthcoming, reserved instead for another time and place.

As we continue eating, we begin talking about everyday things: the economy, immigration, the weather. Of the three brothers, only Bennet and Steve remain in the business. Even though they lived two different experiences during the dark history that is World War II, I still see an intense bond fusing them, strong as silk thread. Their unique connectedness forces its way into my consciousness with a kind of reverence. I think of Kalvin and wish I could meet him, know him. The idea of Kalvin that began this most lucrative of businesses is physically absent but surely his legacy lives on in these two men's devotion to one another.

It is impossible for me to not feel compassion and incalculable respect for the three brothers—their efforts, their gifts, their knowledge, survival, and overcoming of a painful past. For they have made contributions to each other's individual lives, their children's lives, to Los Angeles's garment district growth to be sure, and ultimately to all of us, as survivors of the Holocaust. They are examples of what it means to live, to strive to succeed against all odds. It does not escape me that the noblest parts of their examples remain, and I recognize all the while the great, good fortune I have to be their witness and communicator, however humble my attempt.

All these thoughts I digest along with the sandwiches we share. Steve sits on one side of the table, Bennet the other. Then, eyes down, Bennet reaches to pull my empty plate away, in an effort to tidy up before we leave. And I am reminded of the remarkable journey these brothers have made in their lives; from the remote village in the Carpathians to downtown Los Angeles, poised from the early days of their factories and commercial endeavors, challenging us all by their focused determination and grit. Life, it seems, is about far more than mere survival. It is acting on your own and your brothers' brilliance and belief, in an effort to create more meaning than you ever could have imagined.

# CHAPTER 24

Meanwhile, at home Laura and Leonard were growing, but things were not getting better with Carole. Not only did she not get along with me, but she also was fighting with Kalvin and Steve. Because of our fights, I was the first to open up the factory and the last to go home each day. Carole's mother would come to visit us, and go home crying, she would be so upset by her daughter's behavior and our deteriorating marriage. Carole was just a very unhappy person whom no one or nothing could ever satisfy.

In 1963, we went on our first vacation, an inexpensive trip to Mexico. It was there that Carole got pregnant. We only realized that she was pregnant when she was in her third month. I felt that our kind of marriage could not last much longer without my having a nervous breakdown. I was concerned about the situation and having a child under those conditions. There were no easy solutions and so, on April 28, 1964, Linda was born.

By then we were living on Swall Drive. Now, in addition to working hard in the factory, I worked at home—washing diapers, mixing and heating formula, getting up at night to tend to the baby, and emptying the dirty diapers that were waiting for me on the toilet tank. Sometimes at night I would have to get up to buy Carole a cream cheese sandwich or an ice cream.

Both of us were very unhappy, fighting all the time. In short, we had a miserable marriage. I know that the children suffered, too. I think that living in a difficult household caused Laura's asthma. I finally suggested that we go to a counselor, or perhaps to a rabbi. Carole did not want to go to see a rabbi because she felt he would be biased in my favor because I was a cantor. I was exasperated and said, "OK, then, let's go to a priest." When she didn't like that idea, either, she decided that we should speak to a marriage counselor. She found one on Sunset Boulevard, and we each saw him separately, I after work, and she during the daytime. After several sessions, the counselor confessed to me that he couldn't understand how I had withstood this life for so long. I replied that we had three children, and that if the situation could improve, I wanted the marriage to last.

When we were ready to have a joint session with the marriage counselor, the therapist told me that it shouldn't have been my responsibility to get up at night to buy ice cream or sandwiches. Carole was home during the day and she could have shopped for these items and treats. The counselor pointed out a lot of problems in our relationship. Finally, he said something that Carole didn't like. She stood up, told him that he was crazy, and walked out.

That was the end of our counseling. Our life together got worse and worse. The children were nervous, I was upset, and Carole threatened to divorce me. In 1966 she served me with papers and changed the locks on the doors. When I came home, nobody would let me in. I spent the night at a motel on La Cienega, and found an apartment on Reeves Drive the next day. However, when we went to court for the separation, the judge ruled that our house was large enough for me to stay in one room. This meant living in hell for me. Carole flung my things around and threw my photo album and charcoal drawings that I had made for the kids into the garbage. I was able to salvage the album by going to the garbage dumpster in the alley and digging it out from under the mess.

She humiliated me. The kids were afraid of her and consequently did not talk very much to me, afraid of her wrath if they got too close to me. She charged such great sums onto my credit card that I had to place an ad in the paper saying that I was not responsible for her debts. I took some of the new items that she had hidden under her bed back to the stores. I still tried to talk to her, to reason with her so that we could work out our problems. I paid for her to go to a psychologist and we even made up for a short time—I told my family that we had reconciled our differences.

However, our reconciliation lasted only two days. Finally, I moved out. She went through three different lawyers by the time our divorce was finalized.

I wanted to settle out of court because she had indoctrinated the children against me. I didn't want the kids to resent me so much that they would testify against me. Our settlement required me to give her $400 a month, in addition to $300 for child support. This seemed like a lot of money to me, but Kalvin advised me to "pay her whatever she wants—just get rid of her." The children were to visit me every other weekend, and we were to have dinner together every Tuesday and Thursday.

As it turned out, I had the children with me almost every weekend, because Carole was always going somewhere. She often trusted them with an 85-year-old woman, who was hard of hearing and who would warm up the house by turning on the gas stove. I could not stand this, so I would have the children come to be with me instead.

"You were married for how long?" I ask Bennet.

"Fourteen years—eleven of it in New York, about three here in L.A.," he tells me.

"Why didn't you leave sooner?"

"Well, like I said before, there was very little divorce in my family. I came from Europe and it just wasn't common. And I kept thinking, 'it will change; she will change.' I had three jobs in New York. She always complained that I didn't make enough money. She had no sense of proportion, no common sense when it came to money."

"And the marriage did not ever get any better when you came to Los Angeles?"

"It got worse," he says, biting off his sentence, tightening his lips, digging in.

"And even though you were making far more money here, it wasn't enough?"

"No."

"And while you were working very hard here, too, you were also gone a lot, yes?"

"Yes, she complained about that. But I had to work hard." There is cloud cover in his eyes now.

The tension in the room permeates our atmosphere. I feel the ghost of Bennet's bad marriage hauled in, like so much toxic waste, and I think of my own marriage as it deteriorated. And while he keeps so many more details of the conflicts to himself, forever hidden, I know that no one person "barks at the wall" alone. Fault lines of marriages are always shared.

"And you stayed so long because of…"

"The kids," he says interrupting me. "They seemed hard for her to parent. Linda was two, three years old. I kept thinking about the kids," he says swallowing hard. I can hear his throat.

Many a marriage has lasted beyond its shelf life because of kids. The strategy becomes delaying the inevitable for a multitude of reasons, but always looking into a child's eyes and knowing that leaving them, rupturing their world, will have its own pain. It takes a while to see that for some staying is worse. Marriage disintegration has its own ground zero but, sadly, the disintegration happens in slow motion, much like regaining consciousness after anesthesia.

I imagine, too, the confluence of systems—the ferociousness required of a burgeoning business enterprise with the brothers, the focus on extended family that is clearly at odds between Bennet and Carole, and the dramatically different cultural perspectives between a European Holocaust survivor and an essentially comfortable middle-class New Yorker, that undoubtedly primed the most perfect of storms. Maybe it was doomed from the start. One thing is for certain; doomed or not it was unseen as such at the point of "I do."

The echo of "what would you go back and change in your life" presents itself to me now: the marriage, Bennet has told me, on more than one occasion. How lovely, hindsight; how cloudy always is forward vision. "I did not like the person I became in my own bad marriage," I say and while he does not identify that as his experience, am I catching a thin veil of familiarity covering his downcast eyes?

He continues staring impassively from the couch, and it seems that this chapter in Bennet's life has its own hardness: Not the camps' hardness but this chapter is nevertheless a carrier of its own emotional brutality. The man always seems to be losing family in one fashion or another. I wonder if fear of that loss, consciously or not, entered into the decision to continue in an awful situation even if it made little sense to stay otherwise. And I wonder, too, if his enduring toughness learned from his earlier years allowed him to endure more than most people ever could have, and maybe more than he should have.

I wonder.

Bennet continues sitting, when quite suddenly no small amount of energy storms his face. The atoms in the room have shifted yet again. A new configuration has emerged as he turns to me and says briskly, "Want a bite?" as if to say, we are done here.

"Yes," I say weakly, but with great relief, and then a firmer "yes," seeing sadness but also a dignity that preserves hope that lies buried beneath his sorrow; that even overwhelmed by the death of a marriage, he is never far from the phoenix in him that undoubtedly will rise again.

After all, Bennet has learned to recover from things, even though it may take a while. You will see. Recovery does not mean you don't have initial messiness; it does not mean you connect all the dots right away, either. Recovery means, struggling as you may, and while licking your wounds, you find a way to put one foot in front of the other, continuing the forward momentum into your own future.

■

# CHAPTER 25

In 1967 our divorce was final, and Laura came to live with me in my apartment. She had run over to my place because Carole had almost choked her, beating her for an apparently minor reason. Somehow we managed to live in my one-bedroom apartment, though I knew that I would have to buy a house, since I guessed that the other children would be joining us, too.

At Carole's house, the children never found enough food in the refrigerator. They ate well only when I took them to a restaurant or prepared dinner at my own place. Carole was supposed to buy clothing for them, but I always had to do this. I pleaded with her to let Leonard and Linda come to live with me also, but she refused. One evening as I dropped them off after dinner, Linda cried that she did not want to go home. Carole stood in the doorway, smiling sarcastically. Finally, she announced to Len, "Tell your father that if he gives me the check right now, then you and Linda can go to stay with him."

She wasn't due to get my check right then, but she had spent all her money. She never could manage her funds, and liked to shop at the most elegant department stores.

She'd also have food delivered to the house. After we got divorced, she spent Leonard's bar mitzvah money, sold the piano that I had bought, and sold a ping pong table that I had gotten for Len. But when I heard her words that evening, I wrote out the check for her, and the children came with me. Laura was then already in college, Len slept on the couch, and Linda had to sleep with me in a queen-size bed.

In a few weeks I found a house on La Peer Drive, one block from where the children used to live. They could continue at the same schools. I paid $57,000 for the house—more than it was worth—because I did not want to disrupt their daily programs. The house had two bedrooms, a little maid's room, and one bathroom. Because I wanted Len to have his own room, we converted the garage into a room with a shower and toilet (I remember that this cost $7,500). I had to build a carport because there was a law in Beverly Hills that required every house to have a two-car garage and I only had one.

I moved most of my furniture by myself, and hired a Mexican housekeeper named Maria. I was happy that the children were with me, even though the tasks were so hard. I would look at them as they slept and just cry, sad that they would no longer have parents living together, married. Sometimes Linda would call her mother, asking if she could sleep over there. However, Carole usually came home around nine o'clock, after Linda was already asleep at my house.

After the kids came to live with me, Carole sold the house we had lived in. I continued to pay her mother every month, since we had borrowed $5,000 from her to purchase the house. I paid alimony for fourteen years, which is the length of time that we were married. Carole sold everything that she could, and then traveled. She went to Europe, Africa and Asia, but she couldn't even take the children for one weekend to Palm Springs.

About a year after the divorce, we had a conversation about treating the children well. She asked me to spend some time with her, to take her to a movie. When Laura found out about this, my daughter grew very upset, and complained, "Now you want Dad to take you to a movie? When he was home, you made his life miserable." Carole had thought that people would be attracted to her now, but reality hit when nobody stood in line for her.

Each year I took the children on vacation. They were much happier now than they had been in a home full of strife. Len liked to play the drums with a group of friends in his room; the playing did not disturb anyone. Laura, who was a good student, attended the college at Northridge, studying to be a teacher. In the summers she worked at the factory. Laura got married to a very nice young man, Rick Plasse, who was a medical technologist that she met while a student. I grew very fond of him over the years.

Leonard did not like school very much. He wanted to go out of town to college and was accepted at the University of Colorado in Boulder. When he left, I told him just to concentrate on studying, and not to worry about food or clothing. Within a year, he was an excellent student. He was popular and was still friendly with boys who had attended public school with him. Linda graduated from high school and went to live with Laura and her new husband, Rick, and studied at a beautician school. When she got a job in a beauty shop, I would often drive out to where she worked just to get a haircut. Eventually she came back home to Los Angeles and got a job nearby.

We will tackle the kids later on. Instead I set my sights on his wife.

"Did you have much communication with Carole after the kids grew up?" I posed.

"Not really, no, but once in a while. Sometimes I would give her money. She had a problem with that always. I saved her from several catastrophes." he tells me.

"Sometimes, too, the kids didn't want to see her when they were older, or for her birthday, or even to send her a card or present. I would tell them, 'she's your mother no matter what; you have to send her a card'" he adds.

"I understand she passed away a few years ago. In 2005? Did you see her before she died?"

"Yes, she had stomach cancer and was in the hospital for weeks. I went almost every day and would just sit."

"What did you talk about? Did you ever talk about your past with her, about yourselves?"

"No, we did not talk about us. We talked about the kids, ordinary things, you know, what was going on currently, things like that."

You only spoke of ordinary things?

It is clear that she will always be the mother of his children and I reflect on his own mother's death. I wonder if they connect in

Bennet's mind but do not ask. Instead, I sit in the moment, regarding him, looking at his eyes as they look out at the street, always clearly. It seems unimaginable that Bennet would have acted in any way other than to visit Carole, to extend compassion to this woman even in the face of past suffering while in a marriage with her. I'm not sure I could do this kind of vigil. It may be, too, that sitting in her hospital room afforded him an opportunity to examine himself. There may have been a kind of resolution or restitution going on in its own way—for both of them, I suspect, albeit silently.

And one more thing: sometimes actions possess power and force that words can't touch. As I watch him, his expression tells me what his mouth cannot. His expression tells me there is a place in both life and death that speaks to forgiveness regardless of who wronged whom, and that compassion speaks loudest of all.

So I do not press him further. I will respect his limits that he preserves for Carole's family still living, his own children, and likely himself: he will not reveal too much.

The moment passes and while I am denied deeper details of their married life, I am aware that once the breathing stops, so does the guilt.

"Have I ever told you that sometimes I think I've made the best mistakes I could make in my life?" I say and laugh.

"I think you have," says Bennet, rolling his eyes, his mouth upturned in the slightest of smiles.

"My own marriage was a mess, but I was a mess. Sometimes my mistakes have informed me about myself," I add. How else could I have seen certain things? And while mistakes can be oh-so-incredibly-painful, at the end of the day, the value of the insight that grows out of their examination far surpasses pain. There is no tragedy in making mistakes and having to learn lessons. None. Tragedy only remains in not learning them.

Bennet lifts his head, pointing it directly at me, but not speaking. In an instant, I am reminded of how brave Bennet has always been. His courage just keeps presenting itself in one form or another throughout his life.

Even now.

■

# CHAPTER 26

For a year after my divorce, I was very despondent. I had been the one to get up at night to tend to the baby, so I was always worried about the well-being of the children. I lay in bed one night, feeling sorry for myself. I knew that my life was just not satisfying. I recalled that when I had still been married, we had had dinner at a restaurant called The Four Tree Restaurant, on Sunset Boulevard, and I had noticed how the people were enjoying themselves, singing and having a good time. I remembered that there had been a piano bar, and that the pianist played all kinds of music. Right then, I decided to make a change.

One night I went to the restaurant for a bite. I waited around and began a conversation with the piano player, a Hungarian named Emilio. When I told him that I could sing, he got up and announced that "an opera singer is going to perform now." I hesitated, but after a lot of urging and clapping, I sang a few Italian songs. From that moment on, I did not have to buy my own drinks. But even though the drinks were lined up before me, I didn't have more than two.

As I stood at the piano, a waiter passed me a note, inviting me to sit at a table nearby with two women. I was embarrassed because I didn't know exactly what this meant, but I obliged. The women introduced themselves. I told them my name, and we had a drink. The older woman was a secretary in a bank; the younger one, Paula, who was about twenty-eight, told me that she didn't work. We talked for a long time, and when I left I asked the younger woman for her telephone number. She said that she would prefer to call me instead, in a few days.

I waited for more than a few days, very anxious to hear from her. Paula was the first woman I was interested in after my divorce. I liked her sense of humor, and she was pretty. Finally, after two weeks, she called me, saying that she would pick me up and that we'd go out to eat. I waited in front of my apartment, and we drove to Santa Monica. Paula told me that she had been divorced for a few years, had worked in an oil company office, but had quit her job a few weeks before. She did not want to tell me where she lived or what she was doing now. I didn't pry into her private life because she said that she might tell me more someday. I told her my own life story, and she drove me back to my place. When I asked her if she would like to come in, she replied, "Maybe next time."

The next time arrived, and this time Paula told me more about herself. She had originally come from Arizona, and had been working in an oil company office. Her boss, an important official in the company, fell in love with her and promised to pay all her expenses so that she did not have to work. He was married and had three children, and his relationship with her had been going on for quite a while. She agreed to continue with him because he promised to marry her one day. But he could only see her when he went on business trips or in the afternoons. For the rest of the time, she was very lonely, especially on weekends.

We became involved, and Paula told her friend that she wanted to move to Beverly Hills (she was thinking that she would be closer to me). Up until then, she had lived in midtown, so it was a long trip for me to get to her place when the coast was clear. She moved four blocks away from me, and anytime her boyfriend left, she would call me and I would walk over. Paula also had a good lady friend who knew this man, and whenever her boyfriend was looking for her, this friend knew to call her at my place.

This was a good arrangement for me because I was in no position to have a serious relationship. She built up my confidence, especially when she expressed wonder at the idea that someone else could have let me go. She regarded me as the most intelligent, caring man that she had ever met, and we had a terrific time together. Once, we went to Las Vegas. On that trip, she called her mother, who informed her that her boyfriend was looking for her, so we took the next

Of course I am intrigued by this whole story, having had my own risky dalliances after a divorce.

"How long did this go on, this first affair?"

"Well, about a year and a half, maybe two," he tells me.

"Was it exciting? It must have been exciting," I press, thinking of my own thrilling affairs.

"Well, I guess it was, yes," he admits. "And like I say, she built me up after I had been so miserable in my marriage. I used to think maybe something was wrong with me. She would tell her friends how great I was. It was good; she was good. She was kind and caring. Here I'd found a lady who thought I was great. She took care of her mother, too. She was a nice person," he repeats.

"Did you love her?"

"Yes."

"But you didn't want to marry her?"

"No, I was in no position to marry her, but she wanted me to."

"So she loved you, too."

"Yes."

"How often did you see her?"

"Usually about two or three times a week," he says. "One time she took me by his house and showed me where he lived. It was a big house in Westwood."

"How did this romance come to an end?"

ex-husband. However, he commented that my face looked familiar, and that he had seen me in the restaurant. She denied this. One day she suggested that we get more serious and that she would leave this man, with the idea of marrying me someday. But I wouldn't hear about a committed relationship—and definitely wouldn't hear about marriage—so she dropped the subject.

Meanwhile, I bought the house on La Peer, and she would help me shop and cook dinner. One day, she had a fight with the other man, over his procrastination. She finally admitted to him that the man in the photo was indeed Bennet the singer, and that she was going out with me. He grew furious and threatening, but I had no idea about this turn of events. One evening in the restaurant, he walked in with her. He came over to me and queried, "Do you know Paula?" I replied, "Yes, I see her sometimes here in the restaurant." She tried to pull him away. They had dinner and a lot of liquor. I waited for them to leave before I exited a few minutes later.

As I left the restaurant, I saw him parked in the front. As I walked on the sidewalk, he jumped the car onto the curb, and tried to run me down. I leaped over a little hedge, and he drove off. This experience really scared me, so I told Paula that I had three children and could not afford to have a fight with this man. I informed her that I could no longer see her. The other man also got hold of my phone number, and used to call me at odd hours to find out where Paula was. I threatened him with a call to the police if he continued to harass me. Eventually he divorced his wife, married Paula, and they moved to Phoenix.

"So it ended."

"Yes, it ended," he confirms. "Towards the end, he used to call me, drunk and crying, saying, "I love Paula."

"He did this for about a month," Bennet adds. "That was around the time I told him to stop calling me or I'd call the police. He never called me after that."

"Do you ever look back and think about some of the things you've done in your life and wonder why?"

He laughs a little, the self-deprecating kind that acknowledges the silliness, but then says, "I was young; she was beautiful; she made me feel good."

"I guess so. And you were vulnerable," I add.

"I guess, but it turned out to be a dangerous liaison. I don't think I would have done this if she had come along later," he says.

Probably not. First affair after a marriage—many of us have done it. Some even marry "it." Bennet was wise enough to see this much.

"One time after they moved to Arizona she made a trip back here to see a friend," he told me. "She wanted to see me, so we got together. She called another time, too, but I told her 'no.'"

Like his turtles outside, I pull my neck back into myself after this final statement as I gaze over at Bennet's face, trying to picture him having carried on this way. It is the stuff movies are made of, his life, yet so ordinary at the same time. But always, always it is the aliveness he insists on, and I marvel at the man in front of me, neither humble nor proud, I'm thinking, just so much chutzpah.. So demanding of life, even if he trips, always getting back up, correcting what he can, moving on to the next thing, the next step.

Quite intoxicating, really.

# CHAPTER 27

Meanwhile, Kalvin, Steve, and I worked hard. Eventually we established two factories. The large one—where Kalvin and I worked—was called Mermel & Mermel; the smaller one, called Julie K, was Kalvin's son Howard's responsibility initially. Steve managed it later. Sometimes, Kalvin and Steve's personalities clashed, but I got along with both of them. And we were decent about everything. If we had an argument, it remained in the factory. As soon as we left the offices, everything was forgotten. We did activities together practically every weekend.

In 1978, there was a huge tragedy: Kalvin had a heart attack and died. We were devastated, especially me. I could not believe that he had died so young. We had been together nearly every day. On weekends I used to go to his house to swim at the pool. Everyone who knew him loved him. All the workers adored him. He had enjoyed life, loved to play cards, and loved to live.

Kalvin's family was also, of course, devastated. His wife, Ruth, lost a devoted husband. Howard worked in the business, and Dorothy was scheduled to be married just one month from her father's death. It was a very difficult time for everyone.

After the eight-day mourning period, I went back to the factory, but broke down and could not enter the workplace. My thoughts were of Kalvin. He had told everyone how we struggled in the concentration camp, and how I saved his life.

Today on the couches, in my mind I hear a song as I wait for Bennet to settle. "He saved my life; he saved my life," Kalvin's rhythm echoes.

For Bennet's part I hear his half of the duet: "Sometimes I gave him some of my bread or soup with potato because I knew he was weaker." And I think, too, of the time when Kalvin wanted to give up on one of the death marches: "I can't go on. I want to lie down; just leave me here."

The ghost of the man pivoted Bennet's life when he died. Kalvin pivoted Bennet's life when he was in the camps as well. Would Bennet have turned out to be the man he has become had it not been for Kalvin? I see in Bennet a protector born early, yes by chance, but also by choice, to save a brother. It has occurred to me more than once that while Bennet kept Kalvin alive, Kalvin kept Bennet alive, for he gave Bennet a mission, a purpose larger than himself that transcended beatings, starvation, brutal abuse, everything.

One day, Kalvin threw himself down in the gutter and said that he did not want to live any longer. An SS officer quickly pointed a rifle at him, ready to shoot. I grabbed Kalvin and pleaded with him, saying, "You see the light there in the distance? That's where we are going."

"Did Kalvin know he had heart trouble?" I ask.

"Yes, he had had a mild heart attack previously."

"What exactly happened in the end?"

"It was around eleven at night. Kalvin had been out with a friend for a late supper of pancakes and was on his way home. He had his heart attack on the corner of San Vicente and Wilshire, lost control of the car and plowed into the Big 5 store wall."

Bennet has suggested that Kalvin did not take very good care of himself. Had Kalvin thought "if I can survive the camps, I can survive anything"? Maybe he felt invincible. One thing is certain: that while Kalvin might have had a mechanically flawed heart, the soul was sound. "He was kind and generous," says Bennet. "Everybody loved Kalvin. Kalvin had a good heart."

"I understand what happened to Kalvin, but tell me what happened to you," I ask gently.

He sits, quietly, not moving a muscle, not even a twitch, and his eyes clear, staring. It seems Bennet has learned to carefully place that mass of feelings in a special private spot. I imagine it to be in a corner of his heart, well protected and cared for. What else could he do?

"I was very close; we were very close," he says, simply. "He was such a young man and it was a terrible loss. His death was hard for me to believe." Quietly, he adds, "I was heartbroken."

"Because he had survived the camps? He had already survived so much?" I ask, quietly.

"I suppose, yes," he surrenders, softly. "It's always hard when you lose a brother."

"Yes, but this brother is not just any brother. This brother was with you in ways other brothers were not."

I look closely at his face, trying to hold back my own tears, while I stare back at his. There is so much honesty in Bennet's eyes right this very second, revealing a purity of love that is breathtaking, unconditional.

"Did you keep any mementos of Kalvin's?" I ask, in an effort to lead his sadness.

There is the slightest of pauses, a fraction of time elapses, yet I am aware of how huge and magnificent this moment is when he says, "I have his shoe."

"His shoe?"

"Yes, the police gave me a shoe he wore that night. I put it in the trunk of my car. The shoe has been in all the car trunks I've ever owned since he died," he says, wiping his eyes.

It takes great effort for me to hold my breath, as I feel the magnitude of a thousand hearts breaking.

"I have his sweater, too," he adds, nodding towards the stairs where the sweater undoubtedly lives. "Sometimes I wear it."

"But the shoe. Why do you keep the shoe in your trunk?" I ask, sitting straighter, tightening my chest.

"I can't throw it away," he shrugs, adding "it's a part of him."

And Kalvin's a part of you.

"I showed it to his son, Howard, once. He was amazed."

The richness of this emotional territory stuns me and I spot the drain in Bennet, who lost a beloved brother. I also see the fullness of what that brother was for him: love filled to overflowing.

Later in the day, I am reminded of my recent trip to the Holocaust Museum. I think of what their shared experience of survival in the camps must have meant. Surviving the Holocaust altered their connection for life, amplified it even. Through the museum's lens, I envisioned Bennet and Kalvin wearing the striped uniforms of prisoners; I saw them not just as tribal glue but brother glue, cementing their bond in incalculable ways. The smell of the cattle car on display tinged my nostrils when I pictured the brothers amidst a hundred others crammed together, standing ankle deep in human waste, clutching each other. When I looked at the pile of spoons, the cups and bowls, I pictured Bennet scooping a potato and placing it in Kalvin's mouth, urgently saying "eat this."

In my mind, I saw Kalvin symbiotically chewing not only for himself, but also for Bennet. I saw Kalvin chewing for his unborn daughter and the son he will raise once restored to the ranks of humanity and decency. I even went so far as to wonder "Could this spoon on the edge here, this cup just there, have been Bennet's very spoon and cup from which he sustained Kalvin?" It became evident to me that you don't endure an experience like the Holocaust with kin tethered to your heart without that heart subsequently breaking in the most painful of ways, once that brother leaves the planet for good, many years later.

"I could not enter the workplace."

To return to his work life without Kalvin would feel like an amputation, a phantom limb that still feels pain. Of course, there's the obvious "life can end in an instant." But Bennet knew all about life's fragility long before Kalvin died; he knew about it at Buchenwald and Crawinkel and the rest of the hellholes Hitler created. No, Bennet's inability to enter the factory after losing this brother, I suspect, was as much about restructuring his interior world, as it was about grief. Kalvin's death was an earthquake of seismic proportions and was not one death, but two.

In his book *Man's Search for Meaning*, Auschwitz survivor Victor Frankl suggests the necessity to reconfigure life's meaning when the context is changed. "We were together nearly every single day" explains frequency but underneath Bennet's description lies something else. The brothers shared an experience filled with horror, yes, but also filled with transcendence and joy—because they lived. Quite simply, they shared a frequency of knowledge about life, understanding the key their creation was composed in.

Kalvin loved to live.

I am thrown back to those days of the camps; his poem reverberates as Bennet marches on, originally with Kalvin, but this time alone. It's as if his continued living will become a monument, insisting on finding new meaning with every loss he sustains. The idea of Kalvin remains even as he has been ultimately liberated from the darkness he and Bennet once shared.

Stiff-legged, sunken stomachs, hanging eyelids, sunken eyes,
Heads down, as if ashamed of what happened to men,
Shoes with wooden soles that don't bend,
And we are marching.

Useless knees that stiffened,
Skin and bones are wrapped in a raggedy blanket
Tied in the middle with a string.
There is no waist. It is gone with a growling voice,
And we are marching.

Hoping and not praying,
Will not I be the next to tumble and fall in the gutter to be shot?

Yes, but there is a shoe that lives in your trunk, Bennet. It has mended your tender heart for thirty years, knitting it back together over and over again. Kalvin's shoe connects you, the man in time, with your brother, the man outside of time—and that love knows no time.



A new era must begin for Bennet. It requires reflection, assessment, a digging deep inside to discover the uncharted territory of himself. His new state of being is unmistakable: in the face of such heartbreak, he is even braver.

■

# CHAPTER 28

Bennet's account is revealing in so many ways. The business world he will leave acknowledges great effort on all three brothers' parts, but Kalvin uniquely contributed an intuition towards their shared success.

Kalvin's ideas had helped us grow the business. Whenever we had saved up enough money, we bought more buildings. We bought the corner lot of 14th Place and Griffith (on the block next to our factory), and we put up a 9,000-square-foot building that we rented out. We also put up an 8,000-square-foot-building at 740 East Pico Boulevard which we rented to W. R. Grace. In 1977, we bought a big lot on the corner of 11th and Maple, where we put up a 60,000-square-foot building which later became the alley. We finished the construction on this last purchase in 1978.

We had owned a lot of property. The building on Maple and 11th Street became a gold mine. The big doors facing Maple were hardly used, but deliveries came through the wide doors on the alley. Jobbers used this building, and this was unusual in L.A.. The alley had become such a desirable place that people paid key money just to get in. It was a shame that Kalvin did not live to see the success of this enterprise, because it had been his idea to use this space for jobbers. We had had a little office upstairs at this location, where Steve placed a table and some chairs for us to run the management office. We had bought more land and constructed a fifty-eight-unit apartment building on Kenmore Street and Wilshire Boulevard. This enterprise turned out to be a lemon. Demand for housing had been good, but when the economy began to suffer, we had to lower the rents. Luckily, we also built a 60,000-square-foot building under the same partnership on Crocker Avenue, so we were able to fulfill our deals. Steve was very good at calculating. He was able to get the city to lower the value of our building, so our taxes were reduced. He worked hard to make the downtown so prosperous. We had also decided to make our children partners in most of our enterprises so that they could benefit while we were still alive.

Over all the years, we had had a very good relationship with the workers—never did we have to search for help. If we needed more employees, they would bring over their relatives. Five or six people would be there from the same family. After a year's employment, each worker got a one-week paid vacation. We also had a medical plan for which they would pay one-third and we would cover the rest of the costs. And after someone had been employed for three months, they would be paid for the legal holidays. We had workers from China, Korea, Mexico, and many parts of South America. We employed black people, a deaf English couple who could not find work elsewhere. The Jewish Welfare Department had asked us to help them get settled in a job, and we could not refuse; we supplemented their income for all the years that they worked for us. I even trained their sons for their bar mitzvahs, which they held at Temple Beth Torah, where I was a cantor.

I am proud that our workers were so satisfied and loyal. They would bring us food for lunch—Chinese food once a week. I like burritos, so the Mexican women would bring me special ones cooked without fat or meat. When they would marry, I would sing "Ave Maria" in their churches. There is hardly a church in Los Angeles where I did not get to sing. I even went to Tijuana to sing.

I smell the shift in Bennet. I can almost see his chin raised, leveled into the wind as he leaves one world to enter another.

Yes, I can see Bennet turning yet again and I stand at attention, in awe.

∎

Certainly, travel is more than the seeing of sights; it is a change that goes on, deep and permanent, in the ideas of living.

*— Miriam Beard*

# CHAPTER 29



I am struck by his decision to become a travel agent, when he could have just traveled.

"Why did you want to sell?"

"Because in those days you could travel as an agent on what's called an AD75—seventy-five percent off a regular fare. It was cheap; if I could travel and save money, why not? If I need to buy an avocado and it is eighty cents at one market and it is two for four dollars at another market, do you think I'll go to the one that costs more? No. Travel; same thing," he says, simply.

Of course his logic is sound. Most people I know would still never take a class, get listed as an agent, then wait a year to reap the benefits. For a man who is always in a hurry, it amazes me how he also can delay gratification.

"Most people don't think like this and very few would go to all this trouble," I point out.

"Well, that's some of why this country is in the shape it is, economically I mean," he tells me, lips pursed.

Bennet has spoken.

This, of course, sits in the silence between us because I cannot argue his last point. In principle I agree with him. Still, one thing that strikes me about his logic is his acting on it. Most Americans I know are soft when it comes to saving money. Not Bennet. He describes himself as "frugal."

Frugal, and one more thing; he is enterprising. Is this a result of Mukachevo, the camps, coming to America with not one cent?

"I told a friend I'd bring him business, and then I became a partner. Besides forgoing commission and giving it to charity on the travel I sold, I invested in an agency called Travel Bound. I got my money back when he sold the agency. Later on when I met Dee, she owned three travel agencies and I became a partner with her, too. That way I could also continue to travel at a discount," he tells me. "I got lots of business for her," he adds.

"Dee? Tell me about meeting Dee."

Meeting Dee was much later. In April 1993 I went on a trip to Kenya on a safari and to the Seychelles on a cruise. On the boat, there were four ladies traveling together. We started to talk and I discovered the purpose for their trip. One of the ladies, wanting to get away for a while because she had gone through very hard times during her husband's illness and death, had been joined by her friends. She appealed to me very much from the first time I saw her. Later when we ate together I noticed that she had a wedding ring. I thought that she was married but after talking during dinner I was told that she was a widow, so I felt at ease to talk with her. That's how I met Dee.

"But you had already been selling travel for a number of years before that. How long?"

"I actually sold travel for three or four years but as a partner I continued to have the benefits so I kept traveling. "But things began to change in the travel industry so it became harder; you just couldn't get the AD75 as easily."

"But that didn't stop you from globetrotting."

"Of course not. I love to travel and still take my kids on a yearly trip. I don't travel like I used to, though."

In addition to these voyages, I flew to Buenos Aires, and took a bus trip to the tip of South America. There I boarded a ship to cruise the Antarctic. After that, I flew up north and went on a cruise that went past the Arctic Circle. Another time I flew to Jamaica, where I got on a ship that went to Brazil and up the Amazon. I sailed up the Orinoco River in Venezuela and visited an Indian village built on stilts. I visited the Rio Iguaçu Falls and went to Costa Rica and Panama. I crossed the Panama Canal and cruised the Mediterranean. I have taken the Black Sea all the way to Odessa and to a port in Bulgaria. I have traveled through Turkey, Greece, and Yugoslavia. I even took a three-week cruise with Dee to the Indonesian Islands, including Java, Bali, Komodo, where we saw the big Komodo dragons, Sumatra, Borobudur, and many more sites. Then I flew to the Orient, and traveled through Vietnam, Cambodia, and Laos. I saw the Angkor Wat towers, the bunkers, and the mountain people of Laos.

"I used to take presents for the children when I traveled," Bennet says.

"Like what?"

"I would take M & M's, hairpins, soap, pencils, pens, crayons—things like that. I would take a whole suitcase filled with these items to give to children, sometimes adults. One time a guide got upset with me because he said I would ruin them—the locals—and they would always expect something from travelers. I didn't care."

"What prompted you to do this?" I ask, captive to his efforts to reach out to local people, children in particular.

"When I was little in Zdenevo, travelers would come. They would give little presents like this to children. I *loved* it."

Bennet's happy growl has surfaced, his eyes lit.

"It always meant a lot to me. I know how happy I felt when someone would give me something like this so I wanted to give to little children when I would travel. It is such a small thing but can have such a big meaning for the kids," he says.

"Sometimes, the guide would take me to a school and the teacher would hand things out. I felt really good about this. You know, you live such a short time in this world—why not be nice," he says, simply, his shoulders scrunched up in exclamation.

And of course, he is so right. *Why not be nice?*

Sort of Bennet's version of the Nike slogan "Just Do It."

I traveled to the Caribbean, have visited the Greek Islands. Over the years I took my children to Hawaii, and twice to Alaska, following different routes. I visited Scandinavia, and made my way to Leningrad. I toured Ethiopia, and visited the Jewish people in Gondar. From there we flew to Yemen, saw the first two-story dwelling in the world, and also visited a few Jews who were selling silver goods in the market.

If ever I visited a town on a Saturday, I searched to see if there was a local synagogue. I would then attend services. Indeed, I conducted Saturday services in Quito, Tokyo, and India. I volunteered to conduct services for the Jewish holidays in Barbados and St. Thomas, where I stayed for ten days and paid all the expenses for my flight, hotel, and food.

In 1983 I was in India, where I attended Jewish services on a Friday evening, and was invited along with other tourists for a Friday night dinner. At first I hesitated to accept this invitation, but the host kept insisting, so I went along with the other guests. It was a most wonderful dinner, consisting of about six courses of vegetarian food, accompanied by homemade wine. I thanked my host by giving him a bottle of liquor that I had in my hotel room; I presented it to him when he walked me there after the dinner. And when my friend Dee and I returned to India in 1996, she came back with me to the same synagogue. The same man was there, and after I conducted services, he thanked me for chanting so nicely. When I shook his hand, I told him a few things that I remembered about him and his family. He was so surprised that I remembered, because he himself did not recognize me. After a while, I recalled to him that I had had a Friday evening dinner at his house. He was pleasantly surprised, and invited us again to dinner, along with perhaps six other tourists. We had a wonderful meal, and the occasion gave Dee a chance to see how people lived in India.

"One trip I was on in the Arctic, the Northwest Passage, I met a couple; they were professors, husband and wife," he tells me. "He taught at Harvard but I don't remember where she taught. Anyway, I found them very interesting and nice. Later, after I met Dee we were traveling one time in Indonesia and ran into the same couple. We discovered it was the wife's birthday."

He laughs as he adds, "There was this mariachi band. I asked them if they could play "Guanada." They said 'yes' and I sang it for her. She loved it. Can you imagine—a mariachi band? The couple was very touched when I sang this for her birthday."

I switch gears. "What scary episodes did you have while traveling?" I pose to him.

"Well, one time in Costa Rica I had the chain on the hotel door and someone was trying to enter. At first it was alarming, but nothing came of it."

"Another time when I was in Africa on a safari, I was staying in one of the huts alone. I got up in the middle of the night to use the bathroom and there were big ants—hundreds of ants—all over. I tried splashing water to get rid of them but they would just scurry about but not leave. I could not get rid of them. Finally, I took a candle and walked down to the main room and told them they *had* to move me. There were buffalo along the way when I was walking to my new hut. That part was beautiful." he says.

"And beautiful things you saw?

Bennet moves sideways on his couch, a gentle rocking of sorts, his eyes wistful.

"Victoria Falls are beautiful, beautiful," he tells me, hoping to transfer the full impact of their power on him to me. "Niagara Falls are also beautiful but I think the most beautiful are Angel Falls in South America. The falls are very tall and narrow—breathtaking." he says finally, clearly moved after all these years.

"What are the places you liked to visit the most?" I ask.

"Oh, I loved the Solomon Islands and Papua New Guinea."

"Why?"

"They are so primitive. It is amazing to me how people still live, and they are so remote. There are some smaller islands that you can't even get to unless you know some locals. One time, there was an island in the Solomons I wanted to see. There was a small group of us, about eight, and I had a Polaroid camera with me. Well, I knew the locals never would have seen anything like this so I took a picture and showed it to a man with a Zodiac boat. I told him I could take pictures of people there, so he took us to this island."

"How incredibly clever," I tell him.

"The Zodiac boat is like a rubber, inflatable raft and we had to land on a beach and walk through a bit of water to get to higher ground," he says, getting more and more excited.

"How did the island tribe like it when you took the pictures of them?"

"We were some of the first tourists to go there and they'd never seen anything like this before. They were flabbergasted," he says, beaming. "Through the interpreter, the chief asked me if I was married, and I told him 'no.' Then he offered to sell me his daughter," he finishes, laughing to himself.

"How much?"

"About fifteen or sixteen American dollars," he tells me.

Of course I'm thinking ordinarily this would be the kind of bargain Bennet would love, being the frugal man that he is.

"How old was she?"

"About fifteen or sixteen," he says laughing, adding "it was OK for an old man to marry a young woman and the chief wanted his daughter to go to America."

"Why didn't you take him up on his offer?" I ask him. "It seems so 'you.'"

"I would rather have had the girl I saw in Ethiopia. She was beautiful."

"You men, so easy for a pretty face," I say, teasing.

"It wasn't just her face. She was about seventeen or eighteen and was selling things in an open air market. She had a kerchief on but it was more than that. It was also the angle of her face, how she held herself. It was her beauty but also the whole picture of it. If someone from Hollywood had seen her, she would have been snatched right up." He is so alive in the telling of this story, his pale skin nearly glowing, simply captivated. It is not just the woman, either. The story has pleasure long after the actual event, spreading across his couch over to mine.

Bennet continues with a more sobering story. "There was a woman on the boat in the Solomons that I became friends with. She was a writer, and sometimes sat at the captain's table and would invite me, too. One time on the Zodiac boat when we had reached our launch and were leaving the boat, this woman had a seizure and I pulled her out of the knee deep water. If I hadn't been there, she would have drowned."

So matter of fact, so routine, is his telling of this last little life-saving tale. I let it pass.

"Did you ever get sick on any of your trips?"

"Not really. One time when I was with a group of about thirteen in Africa, we were on a trip down the Zambezi River in a Zodiac boat. They had meat that was not refrigerated, bread, and vegetables. I told the group I was with not to eat the meat. I didn't eat any but everybody else did. They all got sick for days. I was only sick for about twenty-four hours. We were supposed to go on the Blue Train from Johannesburg to Cape Town and had to cancel that, plus reschedule our flights home."

"I always tried to be careful about what I ate when I traveled," he adds. "In China I mostly ate rice. I was very conscious of things," he says.

"Is there any place else you'd still like to see?"

"Yes, I'd still like to see Easter Island and Madagascar. I'll go some day," he adds after a brief private thought.

I wonder. Will he? The desire exists but there may be less appetite for all that it takes to get there.

"You went so many places; you are so fortunate to have done the traveling you did. What propelled the volume of it all?" I ask him.

"I am so curious about the world. Still."

"Did you ever have anything stolen, like a passport?" I ask.

"No, but once when I was in Rome, I caught a man with his hands in one of my front pockets. I noticed him when he first got on the train. There were several of them and I knew they were pickpockets. I had one hand in one pocket and was standing, hanging on to the bar with my other hand, leaving my pocket exposed. The guy moved closer and suddenly jostled up against me pushing, sticking his hand in trying to take my wallet."

"What did you do?"

"I pushed back and said 'I will kill you in a minute' and he backed off."

I'm stunned. Is this maleness talking, this threat? Is Bennet's response more a consequence of his early history with anger coming out from a deep place wound tight, at once immediate and powerful? The man was trying to rob him and I understand Bennet's push-back in an effort to stop this common thief from the act. I've sensed before that there is fierceness in Bennet. It has saved him more often than not and likely is a cocktail of cunning subterfuge, opaque by necessity, having been cultivated during the war and refined for some time after. In this story his more overt self-preservation instinct is naked and on display; he is more an equal in this situation, a situation so unlike those of the camps. Bennet has the freedom to be direct. Still, I'm not sure what to make of this instinct, this level playing field that reveals another side of his nature. In this instance, I cannot help but regard him with a cool but energized sense of wonder.

And then, like the phoenix that he is, my perception of all this travel, this learning from the world and what he makes of it, forces itself into my consciousness. Bennet is wing-spreading once again, not just because he is globetrotting. Rather, it is his insistence on creating new purpose. After commensurate grieving from losing Kalvin, his instinct is to look for the next updraft, ever rising towards what invariably will follow, spread-eagle into this era of his life. It is more than just marching on, although that is true enough. In addition, his life is comprised of one expansion of meaning after another.

Does he know this about himself? Is he aware of what actually is propelling him? I mean in the depths of him?

# CHAPTER 30

Today when we meet I'm curious about other things. "Tell me more about women," I tease. "It sounds like after your marriage and after Paula, you had several relationships, yes?"

During all the years that I was alone, I met many ladies. In 1970 I met Helen at my dentist's office. She was the dental assistant in the office and was nice. Helen was in the process of getting divorced when we started to date. Both of us knew that we didn't want to get married, so there was no pressure. We were together every Wednesday and on weekends. We traveled together to Brazil and Iguaçu Falls, to Palm Springs, and Las Vegas. After five years we parted, but we remained friends and communicated sometimes. After that relationship, I dated other ladies for periods of six months to five years each.

We are looking at a picture album when he shows me a photo of Helen. She looks pretty enough, I think to myself. There are many pictures of Bennet's travels around the world. He has a thousand pictures, I'm guessing. He seems to be a happy man and in his element while showing these to me, all voltage, charged with excitement.

I am curious about one picture and asked where it was taken. "Who can say?" he answers, lost in thought. Some of the locations have slipped from memory but not most. I am on a hunt for a former Bennet, one that includes family, friends, and geography—all ingredients that feed him.

Lifting my head, I see a lovely picture of Bennet and Dee as a couple that I have noticed before. "She is pretty," I say. This relationship was different, lasting longer and likely deeper.

"Yes, she was petite, always clean—she took two baths a day; she loved baths."

I laugh to myself about the tender idiosyncrasies that compose a person and their relationships, and what Bennet remembers of her and is willing to share.

"Dee was a fabulous cook, fabulous. And she had a wonderful personality." He says this last part with emphasis and affection.

"She was a very good businesswoman, with three travel agencies. She was smart and a doer, a wheeler-dealer."

Bennet's mood changes a bit. "She also liked to arrange things in the house. She would come here and try to move things around," he tells me, with no small amount of irritation in his voice.

I wait, watching his face.

"We traveled a lot together; something we both loved to do."

"She lived in Phoenix and you lived in Los Angeles. How did that work?"

"We bought a house together in Scottsdale; I would go there on weekends. Sometimes she would come here but more often I'd go there. I didn't like it when she bought a house an hour from the airport in Phoenix. It was too much. She just wouldn't listen to my wish to have it be more accessible to town, to my traveling there. Her ignoring my position happened too often."

Seems like a long way to commute for a relationship, I think to myself, although for a man who doesn't want to get married again this arrangement clearly had its advantages. Still, the commute wore thin, that much is evident. What is more compelling, however, is the too many times of "ignoring my position."

"What else did you have in common besides travel?"

"Well, we did that a lot but we also had similar views on natural lifestyles, trying to stay healthy. She used to get a little mad when I could do word puzzles far faster than she. And cards, we would play bridge and I taught her to play Kaluki—a sort of European bridge. We'd play Kaluki with my friends when she would come here," he adds, warmly.

"But the travel, it was great. She was proud of me and liked to 'show me off.' She'd tell people I had survived the Holocaust, how remarkable that was, that I knew eight languages, and that I was the greatest singer. Dee used to help me when I would do services on cruise ships or other locations, too, handing out prayer books. She even learned some prayers in Hebrew. She once told me that some of the best times in her life were with me," he says quietly, reflecting.

I turn my head back to the picture of Bennet and Dee, a handsome couple, to be sure.

"So what happened? Why did it end with Dee?"

"We were on a trip to Africa with the kids. She had her granddaughter with her and there was a mix-up in the rooms. She got very upset and I was uncomfortable with how she was handling it in front of my kids."

"Had the relationship been deteriorating before that?"

"No."

No? You break up with someone because of a scene?

I am sniffing out a fundamental conflict of interests here, some unspoken quality that has wedged its way between the two of them, probably over time. I am also sniffing out that this love affair has passed its own shelf life. Between family issues and distance the air has leaked out of the balloon. Still, it is clear Dee meant a great deal to him. Love was there. They remain friends to this day, talking on the phone, he making a trip to see her after she had a recent and serious surgery. The nature of their connection had its own power and force, it seems, and likely still does albeit transfigured into a different meaning and expression. After all, her picture is still in this room where we talk, staring back at us, into him.

■

# CHAPTER 31



Along with other framed documents on Bennet's hall wall hangs a picture of the slab that had been placed at the head of his mother's grave in Verecke. It contains her name, her life statistics, and the verse from the rabbi that was used at the time of her death. Bennet stands off to the side, looking pensive, serious. I can almost smell the European dirt as I lean into the frame.

In the picture, Bennet is turned away from the slab—but with his eyes on it—as if to connect to his and his siblings' childhoods with their mother. The three children—Bennet, Cilly, and Steve—all chipped in to pay for this reverential act; their dedication spreads itself throughout the picture, smoothing out time, pain, creating resolution. It seems as if for a moment, Bennet is transfixed in another dimension. The migration of her remains to Israel connects the past with the present, the family with the tribe.

There are many other things on Bennet's walls: The art he has collected over the years from his extensive travels. The diversity of items is stunning, unique, and curious. He has Hindu prayer scrolls from Sri Lanka, African masks, black and red coral from the South Pacific, and Chinese cut and colored icons on delicate paper. There are jade-carved turtles and a Latin American hand-made rug, among numerous other items. While these things are interesting in their own right, many incredibly beautiful as well, they strike me as serving a higher purpose. I think of Rene Descartes' sentiment: "Traveling is almost like talking with men of other centuries," and, of course, it is inescapable that Bennet appreciates just such a notion.

In the end, all these things Bennet has collected represent not just his appetite for art but, more importantly, for learning, an appetite not just of the tribe but of the man in particular. I noticed this characteristic when first meeting him, how he marvels at nature, the world, and the people that populate it; and he in turn has populated his house with just such representations. His collection conveys a deep and abiding value of Bennet's. His eyes shine with a delicious combination of intrigue, curiosity, and unmitigated joy when he is excited about some new fact or insight that electrifies his whole being. I imagine his enormous appetite for learning and making practical use of it has contributed substantially to his survivability and, of course, to his great pleasure.

Recently, while I was having breakfast with Bennet, his son, Leonard, and daughter-in-law, Deb, Bennet expressed fear that these artifacts would be pitched after he's gone. It is a painful worry that he has expressed before, that his artifacts will all become meaningless and he along with them. After all, these items are as much him as arms or legs, defining something critical that facilitates his navigation in the world.

"It'll all be thrown away," he said, knotted up and leaning forward.

"I don't know why you say that," Leonard tried to reassure him, helplessly.

"Elizabeth loves your things and wants some of them," Deb added. It seems Leonard and Deb's daughter has the same appreciation for art as her grandfather.

Bennet struggled with the confirmation they tried to provide and the subject was dropped, while all of us directed our gaze downward to the food left on our plates. I think back to our earlier conversation when Leonard had told me he collects art on his own travels. It seems the fruit does not fall far from the tree.

How intense is the desire to pass on to our children that which we hold dear, those principals we value, that have moved us and changed how we see the world. So, of course, I see why Bennet fears his items will be pitched after he's gone. He has donated many things already to the Fowler and Skirball museums in Los Angeles that are important for him to preserve. But he wants his children and grandchildren to have even more of the precious objects that represent him and ideas about him. It is like 'mind and heart' food for Bennet, sustenance that has life, far beyond mere survival. It is a Jewish value as well, all this learning and art, an additional reason fueling his desire to pass on the items that represent the values, filled with so much identity.

All this comes full circle back to the family vacation that is about to take place today. Once again, Bennet is taking his children, their spouses, his grandchildren, and even a couple of nephews on a cruise to Mexico. They will all leave this afternoon.

As mentioned earlier, Bennet has taken his children on annual trips all over the planet for more than thirty years and this year is no exception. Yet again, his personal tribe packs their bags, this time for Mexico. It strikes me that he is trying to give them the whole world by this very act, as if to say "see, see what's out there?" From where I sit, his effort is remarkable, and in its purest form, communicates great love for them. The trips are actions that speak. While I grew up having family vacations to Wyoming or South Dakota or Canada even, never have I had, nor known anyone else to have, travel schooling this diverse and far-flung. The globetrotting is breathtaking.

And so I pitch my head to a greater degree to his children—Laura, Leonard, and Linda. Imagine the Carpathian Mountains, a world away, producing Bennet and his kin, struggling through the most horrific of human events, the Holocaust. Then fast forward this man to Beverly Hills, married, divorced, and ultimately raising off-spring who are at a different latitude and longitude—worlds apart in every way.

When I hear somebody sigh, "Life is hard," I am always tempted to ask, "Compared to what?"

—*Sydney J. Harris*

# CHAPTER 32

Alvin Toffler has said, "Parenthood remains the greatest single preserve of the amateur." No one has any experience going into it. In Bennet's case, he lost his mother early in life and had a father who was remote, in part due to his stern demeanor and ferocious insistence on learning, responsibility, and work. And even though Bennet's parents undoubtedly provided solid underpinnings of learning, ethics, and decency in his early years, he did not have the benefit of adult conversations with them once he was older.

From his perch on the couch today, Bennet sits purposeful and steely-eyed. I am struck by the energy required to keep the Mermel family organism moving into the future. The energy is palpable and has lodged itself not only in Bennet, but clearly in his progeny. Both Laura and Leonard possess this same voltage and supercharged sense of productivity. It is a characteristic at once obvious upon meeting each of them.

Linda balances out the ecosystem of the Mermel clan with a style completely her own. She seems calm, even-keeled, and relaxed, filled with a measured common sense of things. I have told Bennet, "You needed her to cool the sizzle so there wasn't too much spontaneous combustion. You cannot all be in overdrive. Someone has to modulate it." He laughs at this notion.

"Was it hard, single parenting, juggling work, dating, and travel, cantoring on Friday evenings?"

"Nah," he says, brushing off my question. "It had to have been hard, at least at times. It was all hard for me and I only finished raising one child on my own," I say, pressing him.

He seems to be having trouble looking in my direction, staring down with his arms crossed, quietly.

"Okay, tell me the easy parts. Just who are these children of yours and what did you want to teach them?"

"Education, education, education?" He tells me, in a serious but happy blast. "Where would I be if not for education?" he has posed many times.

It seems learning is a responsibility—pleasurable to be sure—but a responsibility nonetheless, in Bennet's worldview. He is a force to be reckoned with—a tornado in a bottle if there ever was one. What must it have been like to grow up with such a teacher? Just as importantly, what must it have felt like for Bennet to shoulder such a disproportionate share of the responsibility, the weight of preparing his three kids to face the world and their places in it—a fatigue factor to the power of three perhaps?

"Laura came to live with me after the divorce, when she was sixteen. Leonard was about fourteen and Linda was just a little girl. Laura was attending Beverly Hills High. At first, she got herself to school by bus, catching a ride with a friend, walking, or riding a bike. Eventually, I bought her a modest car to use."

"How far away was the school?"

"About a mile or so."

"Did she like school?"

"Yes," he tells me, adding, "I always stressed how important it was and that all the kids should read. Laura became a big reader. She read so much that I had trouble keeping her in books.

"She was always a good student," Bennet continues. "After graduating from high school she went on to attend California State University at Northridge. Eventually, she got not only a bachelor's degree—she wanted to be a teacher—but also got a master's and doctorate in education."

"So your education mantra worked well with Laura," I say laughing. "How about Leonard and Linda?"

"Leonard was different; he didn't like school very much. It was hard to get him to study even though I tried. He was very social and had a lot of friends. Leonard played the drums and they'd play music together, often here at the house. I liked when the kids brought their friends here because I knew who they were with, and where they were."

"How did it happen that he became a doctor if he didn't like to study?"

Bennet is squirming over on his couch. "He always wanted to become a doctor so I told him, 'Listen, if you go to college I'll pay for everything. You don't have to work, just concentrate on your studies.' So he went to the University of Colorado. He didn't want to stay here. I knew that he needed to get away. Once he left here, he became a good student."

I remember Leonard telling me in a previous visit that his dad "paid for medical school for me; he paid for all of it." He seemed insistent in his comment, wanting to go on record to confirm how valuable his father's help had been for his life.

"And Linda?"

"Linda had a different experience," he tells me. "After high school graduation and two years at a junior college, she went to Arizona State University for a year or so, but didn't like it. I told her she had to do something, so she went to beauty school to become a beautician."

"So, Linda had a different path," I muse.

"Yes."

"It sounds like she has her own way of learning in the world." It's almost as if she's the metronome to the family fever-pitch crescendo. A necessary function, I think, but do not share this with Bennet.

And so it seems that Bennet has passed on the most important aspects of learning to each of his children, one way or another. They, in turn, have translated education into accomplishments and professional outcomes that serve each of their unique personalities. Ever the lifelong learner himself, Bennet began his education early in life, continued it in Mukachevo, then extended it to Munich and New York, all the while foraging for every scrap of understanding he could find in his daily world. His children know of his efforts, which seem to have served as invisible rudder to their own lives.

Laura went on to become not just a teacher, but a principal, ultimately becoming Superintendent of Schools in Culver City, California, before retiring. Leonard has a world-renowned reputation as a physician and researcher, and is the Medical Director of the Infection Control Department as well as an Associate Professor in the Department of Medicine at Brown University. And Linda, who no longer practices cosmetology, works in the family management business by day, and spends the rest of her time hammering the education message, repeating Bennet's mantra in her own voice to her children.

"And work, Bennet?"

"Laura worked in the factory downtown."

"When did she do that?"

"She did it in the summers from the time she was fourteen, maybe fifteen. Working was important. I told all the kids they had to work," he says strongly, punctuating the word hard like pounding a piano key.

"Did the other kids work downtown, too?" I ask.

"No, Leonard didn't want to, but I told him he had to get a job in high school, so he delivered prescriptions for a pharmacy instead. By the time Linda was old enough to work we didn't own the factory any longer."

"So Linda didn't work anywhere else?" I press. "You have told me Linda's experience was different, coming to live with you when she was very young."

"Yes," he nods, lips pursed. His posture is tight and I notice him lean forward, like a turtle coming out of its shell. "I always had a housekeeper when Linda was a little girl. She grew up differently from the other two. I had to work and worry about her and I'm afraid I spoiled her."

"But Linda is the only one of your children who works in the family business now, yes?"

"That's right," he answers, softly.

I am reminded of Bennet's earlier life, from the time he was a small child, working, working, always working. And then there were the camps, working from sunup to sundown; then Munich and, of course, New York where he worked three jobs to survive. Once the three brothers started their business in Los Angeles, naturally the hard work continued. Work became an expression of the man beyond mere survival. It was natural and honorable to pass this value to his children, a value that has contributed so much to Bennet's life. He has wanted to see his children benefit from work in their own right; to survive but also to thrive.

Work is what it means to be filled, a satisfaction organically grown, tended, filled with accomplishment and connections beyond yourself, even your family. Work is an ingredient for living—like air. This is what I see in Bennet.

I am struck by the vibrancy of the life Bennet helped create for his children. In their home environment, he tried to teach his children many things—some ideas quite specific, like the value of education and work. Other ideas like responsibility, compassion, and pleasure that he passed to them were no less profound. While not subject to measurement, they remain visible both from early stories as well as current tales.

I recall Bennet telling me a funny story some weeks before the family trip to Mexico recently. Once upon a time there was this rooster who lived on Swall Drive. No, wait, that's not right.

Once upon a time an employee offered a rooster to Bennet who, of course, said yes. Linda was just a little girl, a preschooler, with Leonard and Laura in their early teens. Bennet being Bennet decided to keep the creature at home, feeding it, adopting it as a sort of pet. Well, roosters being roosters, it crowed in the morning, announcing sunrise.

I'd like to remind you this is Beverly Hills, not Zdenevo. Ultimately, Beverly Hills neighbors being Beverly Hills neighbors, someone called the police to complain. After all, they were used to being awakened by high-tech clocks, not poultry.

"What did you do with the rooster?" I asked my Carpathian friend.

"Of course, we had to get rid of it. I found a farm near Olympic and Pico—in those days there were a few left—and took it there. This was in the 1960s."

His face was just so much fun to watch in the telling of his story, all light and sunny, like a glorious California day.

"Were the kids upset?"

"Sure," he said, shrugging. "Linda in particular cried and cried, very upset, but you tell me, what could I do? We couldn't keep the rooster. I promised to take her to visit and that helped until she forgot about it over time."

"Later on, after the divorce and after I bought the house on La Peer, we had a chicken, too. We had the chicken longer, about five months; she laid eggs but they weren't fertile," he adds.

"How did you get the chicken?"

"It was a stray."

"A stray chicken in Beverly Hills—you've got to be kidding?"

"Well, anyway, I used to feed it. She liked twelve-grain bread, but she would come and go from the yard. Once she laid the eggs, I had a neighbor take her to a farm that he knew about."

"Did you have any ordinary pets like dogs or cats, you know, like Beverly Hills people would have?"

"We had a cat and a dog, Rusty. I loved that dog. He could come in the house during the day, but had to sleep outside at night in the dog house with the turtles." All creatures great and small had their places in Bennet's universe.

The dissonance between Southern California and the Carpathian Mountains had to have been great for Bennet; certainly as different as chickens are to dogs. How great the challenge must have been to finish raising three children in this world after coming from that world.

Yet, one of the values Bennet is most passionate about is devotion to family, his to his children, his children's to him. Just the other day Bennet shared with me the notebook in which he wrote down so much of his life story in longhand. From it, he pulled out a letter from Leonard, written to his father in 1992, after a trip to Zdenevo.

> I've thought a lot about our trip together and it will forever have left an impression on me as a person, as an American in a land of opportunities, and as your son with great pride in who you are and what you've done with your life...For all of these, I am grateful, and I can only hope that someday my children will be as proud of me as I am of you.

Leonard. The known dynamics of fathers and sons, the intense weight of expectations, spoken or not, remain difficult to encapsulate. In a Holocaust survivor's case, the pressure the son bears from this identification must be profound, in the areas of courage and bravery, in particular. To learn, and to work hard, and to be your own person, are no easy tasks.

Leonard's early tepid educational experience was a mountain to be overcome, requiring grit and determination. The necessity to improve his grades from a less-than-stellar high school record flashes through my mind. It strikes me that Leonard has had his own reasons to overcome fear and develop courage, creating a belief in himself. And his letter shows that he has benefitted from his father's lifetime examples of courage and commitment, both learned and observed first hand. The perseverance of the phoenix has descended to the next generation.

I imagine Leonard required courage to get married after witnessing his parents' fractured union, as well. Leonard met Deborah when he was in medical school in Iowa. Along with Leonard she has raised two children, Elizabeth and Elliot. The life Leonard has built with his wife demonstrates a continued commitment to family, stability, and the values he learned from his father as having merit and strength.

One step at a time: the Bennet Mermel legacy has descended to the son.

Further, Leonard checks on his father by phone from Rhode Island, broadening the notion of family commitment always. With a schedule that would put another person under, he calls his father; even on his way out of the country for conferences, he calls. Sometimes, too, he stops in L.A. for a quick visit prior to work events, when time permits.

A unique contribution Leonard makes to his dad is giving advice, consulting with Bennet's doctors when medical issues arise. Finally, it was Leonard who orchestrated the family gathering of twenty before the Mermel family vacation to Mexico—knowing how much that would mean to Bennet. Yes, Leonard's meeting his own personal challenges requiring courage, commitment to self and family, one step at a time, seems as natural and forthcoming as Bennet's own life examples.

Of course I am struck always by the enormous courage and devotion of Bennet's eldest daughter, Laura. She has known her own grief, losing her first husband, Rick Plasse, in an accident in 1996.

Having married in college, the couple had built a life working hard. As a medical technologist, Rick went on to earn master's degrees and later, a doctorate—advancing his learning consistent with the Mermel values. I recall, too, Bennet telling me Rick lived with him for a while when starting a new job in the area and even helped take care of Bennet after some surgery years ago.

While out one evening walking their dogs, Laura and Rick were hit by a car, killing Rick. Laura survived, and overcoming her grief reminds me of the enormous sustained hope and belief that she had to draw on—one step at a time. I think back to Bennet on the death marches when I consider the perseverance necessary for Laura to put one foot in front of the other. Her perseverance was breathtaking and she saw it first from her father's early life example.

After putting one foot in front of the other for several years, Laura went on to meet and marry Don McGaughey. Also an educator, Don retired from the Torrance schools as a teacher-trainer in technology; he is a whiz when it comes to computers, phones, and technical equipment. And he is generous with his time, talent, and sensitivity in helping Bennet. Always, he is as steadfast as the rest of them. Though Bennet is not his father, Don is "his father's keeper," operating in the same spirit of family commitment.

"Don is terrific. He has helped me a lot," Bennet told me on more than one occasion, with the broadest of smiles resting contentedly on his face. As a couple, Don and Laura contribute much to Bennet's life. After Laura's retirement as Superintendent of Culver City Schools, she has had more time to devote to her dad. She visits frequently, bringing food, the newspaper, and items for the house. She calls daily to check on him. Her constancy is stunning. Her patience and steadfastness parallel Bennet's commitment to his brothers and sisters. Yes, Laura knows what it means to overcome personal loss and grief, developing the courage to rise again, all the while with a devoted eye directed at the man who showed her how.

Linda: how hard it is to be the youngest. A different kind of bravery is required, one that necessitates surviving loneliness, not to mention filling the shoes of those who have come before, while creating and preserving your own identity. By Bennet's own description, Linda did not have an easy time of it growing up with a thinned-down family structure with a single parent working long hours, cantoring, and gone from home so much of the time.

A few weeks back while Bennet and I were having our ritual lunch, he whipped out a box from the refrigerator. With a sly grin, he opened it ever so gently so as not to disturb it.

"Linda brought me this napoleon. She knows I love them and was thinking of me," he said, tenderly. I thought to myself at the time, yes: the love for her father—affection translated into confection. It was so evident because his face told me he knew it. Linda's affection returned in a box to her father.

After practicing cosmetology for a few years in her twenties, Linda met and married Kevin Fishberg, an electrical engineer. Together they have two children, Justin and Jensen, but the union did not last and after several years, resulted in divorce. Kevin remains committed to his children and still maintains communication with Bennet, in keeping with the family tradition.

As noted earlier, Linda did not remain in the cosmetology industry. She is the only one of Bennet's children who is involved in the family business, working downtown several days a week, preserving the connection with the company the three brothers developed and grew. There have been a number of times when, meeting with Bennet, I have heard her voice through the phone, calling to see how her father is doing, keeping her finger on his welfare.

Linda's role of single parenting two children reminds me of Bennet's efforts so long ago. My own role in the same category necessarily reveals to me the fear that has to be overcome. When you are raising children mostly by yourself, there is a place reserved for fright involving another's welfare much like I imagine Bennet reserved for Kalvin in the camps, and later on, in a unique way, for Linda, as Bennet shepherded his youngest daughter through her childhood.

And even if single parenting is not a "life or death" kind of experience like Bennet had in the camps, it requires courage nonetheless.

Some of it has to do with resources, finances, working, time, etc. But so much more has to do with that visceral gut instinct that is intangible. You know you have to communicate to your children that they are safe, cared for, and that all is well. In Linda's case, her "crying for her mother" that Bennet has spoken of undoubtedly required her transcending that place of fear so her children won't feel a similar lack of security in their own experience.

Yes, Linda overcomes fear and loneliness daily, developing a belief in hope and perseverance—one step at a time—like her brother and sister before her, but from a different childhood context. Ah, to be the youngest of the brood requires courage she, too, witnessed from her father's lifetime examples.

Today once again, I query Bennet, "So, it must have been hard, single parenting, yes?"

After a long pause he lets it out. "Sure it was hard. I felt pulled in many directions." Then, almost testy, he says, "I did the best I could. I did the best I could," repeating himself, searching for understanding.

You don't have to convince me, Bennet, I think to myself.

"It is hard to balance getting your own needs met while trying to take care of children, mostly by yourself, don't you think?" I ask him.

He stares straight at me, hard, a snow squall on his face. No words are necessary. I know he knows, the skin on his face taut, his eyes strong.

"Do you ever think about what you've learned from your children?" I continue.

He seems at a loss. "What do you mean?" he utters, blowing out air.

"I mean what you've learned about yourself?"

There is observable squirming occurring, on both couches actually. Have I gone too far?

Then, "I was too harsh with them," he confides quietly. Gaining steam, he adds more loudly, "I did the best I could. I did the best I could."

As he repeats it I catch the aroma of regret but I have yet to see any serious catastrophe in lessons learned from honesty and the best of intentions. That's all any of us can do or ask for; to do the best one can. It's only when your adult child or some other catalyst leans back into your life that you can understand and appreciate that simple fact with maturity. After all, Bennet's children all ran to him after the divorce—and he wanted them.

I've watched all their faces when in his presence. They encapsulate and mirror a remarkable connection that is symbiotic. It reminds me of Kalvin, this intensity they have for each other. It strikes at the heart of what it is to be a parent and child. Bennet gave to each what he or she needed: love, commitment, guidance.

And the reciprocity Bennet's actions have generated? His children's commitment and love are daily revealed as solid and bankable. They all give so much to him. If there is a currency that love can be translated into, Bennet has wealth beyond measure. What's more, while some of this is innate in all humans, not all express it overtly. It is a job well done, passing on to Laura, Leonard and Linda the notion of family, a love as sturdy and sure as the potato passed from one brother to another.

"I did the best I could" echoes and reverberates. At the end of the day, awkward communication of the messages is only that. Never should the style be confused with the substance. In Bennet's mantras of "education, education, education" or "you have to work," even if it's an imperfect execution of parenting, he has given his children everything he could. It is not money that I speak of, although he has certainly done that generously as well. His commitment to them is breathtaking.

I was too harsh, too hard on them.

Maybe he was too harsh, but there's not a parent or child on the planet that doesn't have a stack of grievances. The trick is to figure it all out, forgive, and move on. Ultimately, the responsibility for all of us as parent or child is to curve the finger back towards ourselves. In the end it is one's own phoenix rising from the ash.

What I focus on is what remains; it is the catch in Bennet's throat, the glint in his eye when speaking of them. And while Bennet has been intensely connected to his siblings from the war experience, it is for his children he has reserved the ultimate mother lode. Bennet stands for many things but probably the most critical is his commitment as a father to give all he had of himself. It is fierce. He grew up in a decidedly different world, one that was brutal but also filled with great love and caring, the love he received from his own parents, his siblings, his surrogate guardians in Mukachevo.

"My children and grandchildren and I never end a conversation without saying 'I love you,'" he tells me. It is oftentimes ritual that reminds us of deep meaning that otherwise might be taken for granted. In this ritual they all participate. In the end, it is his children and grandchildren who provide the most intense meaning in his life, sometimes so much so, he's left speechless in more detailed ways. Yes, speechless!

Indeed, his "I love you" has far more voltage than the words can carry.

■

# CHAPTER 33

There is an old Welsh proverb that states, "Perfect love sometimes does not come until the first grandchild."

"I was so excited when Elizabeth was born," Bennet says, beaming today from the couch. "I had been waiting for a grandchild, wanting one." There is delight in his eyes and strong, purposeful emotion in his voice. "After going through the camps, I never knew it would all be possible, having children and grandchildren."

Family: the intense connection continues like arrows shot into the future.

Leonard's daughter, Elizabeth, is the only grandchild I have not met but I know this about her. She was the first. Pictures reveal a beautiful young woman, but one also bright and already accomplished in her own way. Elizabeth graduated from Vassar College with honors in biology, no small feat, and is applying to medical school, wishing to be a doctor like her father. Additionally, she is working in the lab at Brown University's hospital.

"I went there sometime after she was born. I used to play with her when I visited." I can feel him emoting this, as he tells me.

Turning, he tells me, "When each of the grandchildren was born, I set up a college fund for them. I also paid for primary and secondary schooling when they needed additional resources, for all of them."

For all of them? Are these grandchildren paying attention to this genus and species of generosity from their grandfather?

"So you put your money where your mouth is, when it comes to education, yes?"

"Yes," he says emphatically.

Leonard also has a son, Elliot, whom I met at a barbecue last summer. He seemed earnest, intelligent, looking to be a doctor also, but it is early as he has just begun working on his undergraduate degree at Colby College in New Hampshire. What struck me when talking with Elliot was his desire for his own accomplishment while hoping to mirror or surpass his father's success. He is lively and speaks with so much of the Mermel energy.

Like Elizabeth, Elliot also works. His summer job is making burritos at a small restaurant in Providence, Rhode Island where the family lives. Bennet tells me he's not happy with earning only minimum wage, but tells Elliot he should be glad to have a job. "Yes," I reply to Bennet, "but how great he already seeks to further himself." It is evident Bennet's principles of education and hard work continue in the next generation, unabated.

A week later Bennet, Laura, Linda, her two children, Justin and Jensen, and I are having breakfast at a restaurant in Beverly Hills. At seventeen Justin is thin and wiry, possessing a serious, pensive side and looking like he aches to do good but is not quite sure how. Of course, he has a part-time job, working six hours on Saturday and Sunday as a cashier at a local deli in keeping with the Mermel tradition. Seemingly, he carries things on the inside, much like Bennet himself. Of course he is not without his playful side, loving video and computer games. And pasta. The rebel in Justin orders pasta for breakfast.

Then there's Jensen, Linda's twelve-year-old daughter. While we are eating she pops up and down multiple times, looking for something of interest as we sit on the patio waiting for our food. It seems she can't make up her mind whether to remain stationary, eavesdropping on adults, or spin off in her own energized way, examining her environment, much like I imagine Bennet must have done as a child. Is she foraging for information like Bennet?

There is something reflective about each of Linda's children. They seem to have an acute awareness of their grandfather even in the face of all their current crackling energy. I've noticed this displayed in Linda, Laura, and Leonard as well. It's almost as if Bennet has transmitted a kind of radar into his children and grandchildren, then back again to him—a boomerang effect.

"Papa, I got an "A" on my report," Justin tells Bennet, who whips out his money. He pays for good grades and delivers the currency to Justin's outstretched hand.

"Dad, we went to a Dodgers game last night. It was a benefit for the school," adds Linda, smiling.

Education, education, education.

Some days later, Laura sends me an email that Jensen has written from summer camp in the mountains. It is a creative and hilarious description of herself, running down a hill, written with a self-deprecating humor usually reserved for older children or adults. Already, she is a natural at taking delight in the world. In addition, Jensen likes to cook, and I'm wondering how I might get her to cook for me.

But the chronicling of Bennet's grandchildren takes on a unique potency yet another day when he speaks at Justin's school. The tenth grade class has been studying the Holocaust and Justin has invited his grandfather to share his experience. Bennet, Linda, and I arrive at Summit View West—the school's name strikes me as almost funny. The view of the Holocaust from the West Coast of California and from a summit: an eighty-seven-year-old Bennet who has reached a great distance in time and geography, beyond the camp years themselves.

We walk into the school and I am touched by Linda introducing him to teachers, administrators, and the like. She seems proud with her "this is my dad" pushed gently into each person's awareness.

Then, we are in the classroom and I witness a noticeable shift once the teacher has introduced Bennet, as he makes his way to the front of the class. Bennet's energy has changed. Not just because he is a natural performer, although he is. It is obvious he is comfortable in the spotlight, maybe more so than in one-on-one conversation. What I notice is a purposefulness that he exudes. It is not pride, exactly— rather it seems to be a reclaimed dignity. Yes, dignity, as he defines what survivor of the Holocaust means.

He threads the highlights of his story together in abbreviated version, ending with "tell your mother you love her every day, and be kind to one another," and, of course, "don't ever forget; it really happened." Then he opens it up for questions.

"What was it that made you survive?" one students asks.

"I knew I was strong; not everyone was. People had their own ability or not, to make it. I knew a tall man, big guy, who couldn't make it but I believed most of the time that I could."

"Do you have scars from what's happened?" another asks.

"Yes, I can't stand violence. You can ask my children. I never go to violent movies. I can't stand when there is suffering in places in the world like Darfur, Sudan, wherever."

Yes, scars indeed.

One student draws our attention to the fact that today is Hitler's birthday. I learn later that it is also a Commemoration Day of the six million Jews who died. And Bennet is here, on this day, telling his story.

Bennet is here, alive.

The questions wind down and we move out of the room, down the hall. One student catches up with us and tells of his going to Israel in the past year, seeing the Holocaust Museum there. The student tells of a box filled with wedding rings, adding "It moved me."

I see this on the kid's face, transferring the energy from his face into Bennet's.

And then it hits, slams me; while Bennet's talk has moved the kid, the teachers, his grandson, his daughter, the rest of the students, and me, as always, there is a trick going on before our eyes. Bennet looks and sounds ordinary, average even, but with a remarkable story—one that moves people—from the most horrific event in human history. What is harder to see in someone walking around, living their life as if it hadn't happened—appearing ordinary—is the staggering price that is far from ordinary, peppered throughout the years between 1945 and the present.

Bennet's life began slowly so many years ago, and then, as if suddenly, he transfers what he has become, to his children, his grandchildren, and to all of us—those values he has lived by: education, work, family, charity, and decency. Without a doubt, he moves those he meets and knows, first his inner circle of children, then his grandchildren. And then, by broadening the scope, the arrows fly forth into the future. Bennet is the echo in the canyon of a heart, reverberating in time and space, of the values he holds dear. Justin already knows this. All the grandchildren have begun to live their own expression of those values, slowly, as they make their own way through their lives.

■

# CHAPTER 34

In Israel my brother David helped to establish a kibbutz in Hadera called Gan Shmuel. He invented an orange powder similar to Tang, and on the kibbutz was in charge of the factory that produced this product. He was often invited by other countries to give advice about the product. In fact, the Birds Eye frozen food company invited him to come abroad to work for them, but David was a dedicated Zionist who would not leave Israel no matter how much he was offered. He traveled and provided advice in Brazil, Yugoslavia, and many other countries. He and his wife Raya had two sons and a daughter.

My brother Aryeh's first wife was killed by anti-Zionist terrorists. He had one son, named Yitzchak, with his second wife, Eva. My sister Shary did not have any children. She had been like a second mother to us—cutting our hair when we were small, buying our clothes and shoes. The shoes never fit well, because we never tried them on before purchasing. If they were too large, we would slip in a piece of cardboard; if too tight, we would stretch them.

Esty had no children, either. She had married an older man during the war in Budapest. Hudji had a little girl who perished with her in Auschwitz. Bella had a boy and a girl. Cilly, too, had a son and a daughter—Rutika and Georgie—with her husband Miklosh. I, of course, have two girls and a boy. Kalvin married Ruthy, who had a son named Howard from her first marriage whom he adopted and whom we always considered as our own. He and Ruthy also had a daughter named Dorothy.

Steve and his wife Ella had four girls: Sandy, Elaine, Suzanne, and Elisa. Ella, bless her soul, died tragically at the age of thirty-five from a slow-growing cancer, leaving Steve to raise four small children. I remember going many times to help put the children to sleep, and inventing a cute story about Foxy Loxy. I have told the same story to my own grandchildren. Steve lost a wonderful wife, the children lost a mother, and I lost someone whom I adored. Ella had never let me be alone on Fridays: I had to come to their house for dinner. If once in a while I couldn't be there, I still remember the inflection in her voice as she said, "Benci, Benci?" What a tragedy it was to lose her. After a number of years, Steve went on to marry a wonderful woman, Marsha, to whom he remains married to this day.

Because of tragic losses like these, I still keep asking, "Is there really someone who metes out justice?" After seeing Ella suffer, and after seeing old and young alike suffering in the camps, I have come to believe that there is nobody up there. We are brought into this world, without having chosen to be born. We go through life with ups and downs. For some there is happiness, but for the majority, it is a struggle to get by. This is why I believe that the main thing in life, while we are here, is to be honest, to help our fellow human beings, to be charitable, and to respect the elderly—not just because I am one of them. We cannot rely on "someone up there," but have to fend for ourselves.

I heard the crying and the pleading, and there was no answer. We struggle through life, and if we are lucky and live to reach old age, sickness sets in and we pass on. There is no afterlife. When we die it does not matter where we're put. I even remember hearing my own father say, "When I die, they can put me in the toilet." He was a very learned man in every respect, and my thinking is the same. When I hear people saying that God spoke to them (some even have written bestsellers about this phenomenon), I think that these people should consult a psychiatrist. Many people make a lot of money duping others, especially older people, by telling them that they spoke to God, who will heal them. God has become a big business.

There is no salvation. We all wind up in the same place. Nobody is coming down from heaven to save humanity. We here make the world what it is. If we continue deforesting, polluting the water and the air, not controlling the population level, then the world as we know it will be ruined, and no heavenly body will save it.

I sit with Bennet today after having read the story of his life. "I have heard you talk with awe about nature, about the sun and the moon and stars, how the whole universe's beginning is a mystery. But sometimes you seem like you're mad at God," I say to him. "Tucked into your writing are some important ideas, your values: honesty, helping others, charity, respect. Those things are not about suffering. They are about relieving suffering."

I wait for him, watching his face, listening.

"I'm not *mad* at God," he says, calmly, looking at me, leveling his gaze. "Nothing is here forever, even the sun will die. Everything is bound to die. It seems that we have a few minutes of happiness in life and the rest is struggle and then you die."

"Yes, but what happens when any living thing does die? It continues into another form. It is Einstein's 'matter can neither be created nor destroyed' and even with death something else occurs. Just because we may not know what else occurs, doesn't mean it doesn't occur."

He thinks on this, an unsolvable existential Sudoku puzzle. Then there is a sliver, a thin thread that operates in him with power and force when I hear his next sentence.

"Every day is a gift. I wake up every day, grateful to be alive; very happy when I see the light coming through the window. I did it all. I tried everything. I wanted to experience as much as I could, to cram in as much as I could in my life. I loved to travel, to learn. I love nature, shows on PBS about polar bears or grizzlies. I became a thirty-second degree Mason. I loved the rituals, the traditions, bowling."

His face is shining. At once I am struck by his description just now. It is about living. His living eclipses his suffering. I think, too, about his painting, his fluency in eight languages, his singing. He volunteered as a cantor for twenty-eight years at the Temple in Venice. He also directed a choir. He was and remains a vibrant man, a giving man.

These days, I see him doing his Sudoku puzzles and word jumbles from the newspaper, going to breakfast with his children and their families. I know of his contributions to Shelters for Israel, of his anonymous contributions to other individuals and numerous organizations. He has even told me he'd be willing to give up some of his social security for those less fortunate than he, if he could only find a way to do that.

"Why have you wanted to experience it all?" I ask him.

"I don't know why," he tells me, staring back genuinely puzzled at it himself.

It strikes me that, at least in part, he scrambles to the next experience because he continues foraging for the next level of understanding, the next insight about the world and his place in it, his next piece of meaning, the next awe.

Bennet doesn't know all that he knows, but acts on some hidden knowledge just the same, as if there is some DOS system operating in the background. He is operating from intuition, which is about spirit, not thought. Spirit is about a quality that knows of something else even if there's trouble bringing that "something" into focus.

When I first met Bennet we had several disagreements about his disbelief in a conventional idea of God, his cantoring, and what I perceived to be his lack of faith in a deity. Remarkably, I have come to see his apparent contradiction very differently from my initial view. Through an aggregate of decency in his values, Bennet has made me aware of the molecules of something greater than a conventional idea of God.

"I think we are all connected." This is a statement Bennet made to me early on, and one to which I return. It is an awareness that is intrinsic to his nature. I used to think it came from his experience in the camps and while that is partly true, I now believe it began much earlier. To hold the notion of connection, to know it in your depths requires a faith in something larger than yourself. Name it what you will, God, Frank, who cares?

Did it come from suffering? Or did it come from pleasure and joy? Or, like so much on the earth, did it come from both?

"Do you think you've had more happiness than suffering in your life?" I ask him.

"How can you measure that?" he asks me hard and sharp.

"You've seen suffering but you've also known happiness, yes? Are you happy in your life now?" I press.

After a short gasp, he says, "What is happiness, really? I'm satisfied and grateful for my life. I love life."

His statement is primal, capturing an intensity that, from my perspective, reveals more meaning than the words can hold. Yes, he's known suffering. Yes, it bothers him deeply when he hears of others' suffering. But Bennet also knows a love of life that knows no bounds.

Which is to say, Bennet knows love. And how can that not translate to happiness?

*We here make the world what it is.* Yes, Bennet. It seems I have been focusing on the words suffering and struggling in your writing far too much.

Throughout his life, Bennet has learned about connection to others, its value, and his responsibility to act on that belief. "If we can help somebody, why not?" Bennet tells me. It resonates in my head in part because he has repeated it to me; in part because it speaks to a human connection and level of responsibility that brings him satisfaction. Helping others fills him.

I think back to the movie Groundhog Day, where Bill Murray has to keep living the same day over and over, until he makes better, more generous decisions about living—with decency, respect, and connection. At one point, he dabbles in what can best be described as adolescent extreme misbehavior, thinking there are no consequences to his self-absorbed, narcissistic actions. What happens? He's left unsatisfied, like eating a donut but remaining hungry just the same, from so many empty calories.

Later in the week, Bennet emails me about a program on PBS, his favorite network. It is about "The Evolution of God" by Richard Wright, on Bill Moyers Journal, one of his favorite programs. I watch it, of course, and email him back to say that we should discuss it at our next meeting. I'm feeling a spark, an intuition about so much of how I have come to view Bennet. Life is sacred: a sentence he has uttered to me, usually with a quiet kind of reverence, I might add.

Yes, Bennet, life is sacred.

Are you foraging for more meaning again?

■

# CHAPTER 35

Today is our final meeting, with Bennet on his couch and me on mine. It is the thick of summer and hot. The heat seems appropriate, parallel to what may prove to be a heated conversation we are to have, and I am restless, nervous even.

"So what did you think about the 'Evolution of God?'"

"I liked it," he tells me, offering no more.

"You know what I think, Bennet? I think when you were in the camps you saw the old idea of a God 'up there' as an incorrect idea about God. God was not about justice in any simple way, or about controlling everything with no role for men. You figured out there has to be something different about life and its source."

"Yes, why would the Jewish people, why have they survived all these years?"

"Stubborn?" I quip back.

Bennet has a great sense of humor but he is not laughing. He counters with "there must be some reason."

Maybe the reason is to keep evolving? To accept your own participation.

"Yes," I say, instead.

"Life is a mystery, a big question. There is something, some kind of power," he tells me.

"Yes, and you can call that God, divinity, or Frank, it doesn't matter. What matters is the acknowledgement that you and I cannot create a sunset, that plant over there in the corner, or a violet."

Could God be an organizing set of principles, always expanding to a new level, and we along with it?

"There's no beginning and no end; black hole, black schmole," he says, laughing. "No one knows for sure how it all started. No one knows how or why there is a twenty-four-hour rotation of the earth around the sun." His eyes are bright, engaged, and reverent.

"Do you believe in infinity?" I ask him. I am so very restless, feeling so much energy here—like a big bang is about to happen.

"Yes, although nothing is here forever—except love." Then very quickly as if he doesn't want to go on record, he says "just kidding, just kidding."

Is he teasing me? You can't take it back, Bennet.

"Let me introduce you to yourself. I think you have been looking for a new definition of God or whatever you want to call it since the camps. Maybe you've done it mostly through experiencing life, connections with others that are profoundly felt, and principles of decency that are important to you."

He is staring back at me, with so much aplomb, his chin dropped.

"What's more, you are very intelligent and you can access intuition that is sourced from something else."

And then, of course, I'm thunderstruck because I see that he knows exactly what I'm talking about when out of his next breath comes, "When Kalvin and I were on the truck, going to the quarry, I knew bad things could happen there and told him not to speak Yiddish."

"Of course," I say, holding my breath, watching him.

"But it wasn't destiny: there's no one imposing a will on you."

"No, that's because you knew you were to choose—after consulting your environment, intelligence, and accessing your intuition. You knew that your role was continuous, and that you were responsible for taking the next step: for warning Kalvin."

Not separate from God but part of the whole system, with you in it, Bennet, with you in it.

It is the part about Bennet I have come to see very clearly, his taking of responsibility for his own participation and evolution, the interior school from which he really operates. The travel, the nature programs, the turtles, the squirrels, the people, the work, the appetite for the next insight through experience—all of it speaks to his greater awareness expanding his understanding. It's as if Bennet has redefined God through his subjective experience known to him as his life, leaving Abraham's Old Testament notion in the ditch.

"The clincher for me was during the Iran-Iraq war when both sides claimed God was on their side. That did it for me. How could God be on both sides? It was ridiculous," he says, exasperated.

It's the distortion, the abuse, the manipulation, the contamination of God through extremism that Bennet rejects, not the notion of a power that knows no time, that's infinite and loving, a power that facilitates Bennet's using of his intelligence and talents not just to survive, but to determine how to survive with meaning.

"Life is sacred," he says, continuing. "It is precious. We need to honor it." He is emphatic about this, lips pursed. He says this concretely, strongly, with certitude, mining it from a vein that runs deep.

"If you could leave any additional lasting words that you have organized your life around, what would they be?" I ask him.

"Be nice to your mother." He emits this statement from that original wound, losing her far too early but never forgetting. "I wish more people were righteous, kind, charitable, and decent," he adds.

Then he lets slip, "To be peaceful?" He laughs. "Because there will never be peace."

This is an ongoing difference of opinion between us. We discussed this some weeks back, when the white supremacist opened fire in the entryway to the Holocaust Museum in Washington D.C. I was shocked. He was not. I suppose after going through the Holocaust, he found this incident to reinforce his notion of "there will never be peace." At that time, I told him that's no proof. I asked him "does the caterpillar know it's to be a butterfly while in its cocoon? No, it just goes on about the business of building its cocoon, knowing only after reaching the next stage, what it has become."

Apparently tiring of our dense conversation, he hands me a slip of paper, saying, "Here's some Jewish jokes."

So much of the telling of Bennet's life has been about sorrow and struggle. While pleasure has also been described throughout his story, little has been discussed about his delicious sense of humor. He has humor in abundance. In fact, he displays it in great big gulps, a sign of his substantial smarts and his insistence on unmortifying the pain in life. I believe his humor has sustained him.

His nephew Howard told me a wonderful story a while back. The two men typically have lunch on a somewhat regular basis but one time it had to be postponed because of Howard's travel. Upon returning to town, Howard called Bennet saying they needed to set up a time to get together. "Yes, I haven't eaten since you left. Now that you're back, I'm very hungry." It is the kind of wit that is subtle, dry, and delicious, edible and filled with happy calories.

Bennet and I finish our time together with our own lunch. I have yogurt and fresh blueberries. Bennet is eating matzo and fish from a jar—Jewish food. He is eighty-seven years old now. He continues to walk two and a half miles on his treadmill every day. He watches his diet carefully, too. I watch him while he eats, still so purposeful, and with gusto.

"I want to hear you say it. You've had a wonderful life, George Bailey. I want to hear you say it." I am insistent. He knows the truth of what I am asking.

"Yes, I don't deny it. I've had a good life. When I whistle there's a kind of …" he pauses, as if afraid to let it hit oxygen but goes ahead with, "Contentment."

Oddly, there are no clocks ticking. There is so much silence, as if to make room for his statement.

I sense in Bennet not just an attitude of gratitude but an altitude. Bennet has been through many events in his life, some horrific, some quite marvelous. He has not always been perfect, although nearly perfect as he will tell you. Has he made peace with all of his past? Has he figured it all out, what his life has meant? It is unclear, but likely he's gone a very good distance on both fronts. One thing is for sure. Bennet has been clear about what is important to him: to be honest, to work hard, to give generously, always operating from the connection to others that he feels. He values education and is the ultimate self-made man. He has a fierce belief in family.

Elie Wiesel has given the world many things in his mission to help humanity never repeat the horrors of the Holocaust. "Never forget" is important, without a doubt. But what I witness in Bennet, what he carries in himself is his insistence on living with as much meaning and learning as he can cram into his life. His attempt has been to turn from the death of the camps to the life he helped claim, for himself and his brother. He turns away from Sodom and Gomorrah, and instead directs his vision to the curve of the future, the new definition it holds, the expansion of his experiences, life's best redemption. He humbles me.

It all happens fast, the idea of a man curving into time.

> I wanted to cram in as much as I could.
> I heard the crying and pleading.
> I gave Kalvin my potato.

You are your own answer to the questions and mystery of your life, Bennet. Your continued, sometimes desperate search for meaning, claiming your own dignity, cramming and waiting for the next experience from which to redefine the sacredness of life, has transformed you and, by extension, others. I see your reverence for living, and the source that life springs from. It rests in the beat between the notes you sing. That reverence calmly reveals itself in the instant between cracking the nut and handing it to the squirrel, knowing all along it will accept your gift.

The holiness of life and your respect for it is in the breathing. It resides in the rise and fall of what you take in and what you give out. It is never-ending even when your personal experience here on the planet ceases.

Like Job says, "there is a spirit in mankind." But I do not need Job to tell me this. I see it in you, Bennet, rising and falling, ever expanding. I see you.


La Chaim.

# FROM BENNET:

Where is the time that went by so fast?
I thought I had enough time.
I time myself with good timing
And when the right time is sounded by the time clock,
Is it really the time to do the things I time myself to do
When the time is right before it runs out?

And when does the time get shorter if time is everlasting?
Time has no beginning and no end.
But even so, where did all the time go?
How can I do everything in such a short time?

Since there is time for everything,
Why did I not do everything on time?
Why was my timing so late?

And when time is up, is it really the time to go?
I don't see it coming and going, and fading away.

Well, time heals everything, and if so,
Why that time in and out
There are people who are not healed in time?

A long time ago I did not bother with time,
I thought it was everlasting.
Well, it is, but not for you and me.
For me, the time is now
For this untimely rhetoric about money, because time is money
And time wasted is a loss.
So now since we settled it in time,
I'll be out of it in no time.

As for you, you have all the time in the world.
Use it wisely and state your case.
But in time and in good fashion
So you don't run out of time,
Because time keeps on ticking
And it catches up with all of us.
And that's when time lasts
Forever and ever
In a timeless realm.

# ABOUT THE AUTHORS

**ROSALIE CUSHMAN** has a rich and diverse background in public relations, marketing, sales, performance production and writing. She has worked with authors Mary Swander, PoetLaureate of Iowa, Pulitzer-prize winner Jane Smiley, among others, creating and co-producing *Dames from Ames* for Public Television in Iowa. Additionally, Ms. Cushman has promoted numerous authors, including Garrison Keilor, and co-produced three reunion events with Steve Allen for Drake University. Further, Ms. Cushman has authored a memoir for Iowa State University on Margaret Sloss.

Ms. Cushman has been a reader for Big Bear Film Festival for the past six years. She has written web content for a wide variety of websites as a freelance SEO writer contracted with the #1 search engine firm in America—Wpromote. Additionally, Ms. Cushman was a contributing writer for *FINE Magazine*, the Rancho Santa Fe Website, www.ahharsfnews.com and www.values.com. She has co-authored the memoir, *The Man Confused By God*, with Bennet Mermel—a unique dialogue incorporating Bennet Mermel's life story, spanning his remarkable life of courage and triumph from Buchenwald to Beverly Hills. Ms. Cushman has written two other books, *Vibrating At The Speed Of Love* and *One Grasshopper's Journey*, as well as writing for her own website.

**BENNET MERMEL** began his early life in Zdenovo, Czechoslovakia, developing a love of music at an early age. His education was interrupted by WWII, ultimately surviving multiple concentration camps and numerous death marches, along with his brother, Kalvin. After liberation, Mr. Mermel went on to 'survive freedom,' making his way to Munich to study Opera at the Handel Conservatory of Music and Academy of Music. In 1949, Mr. Mermel immigrated to the US, settling in New York for a time and began building a new life. He earned a degree in Sacred Music from Hebrew Union College, became a Cantor at Flushing Jewish Center, worked as a pattern-maker at Slender Styles, married, and began a family. In 1961, he relocated to Los Angeles, and developed several clothing enterprises, Julie K and Mermel & Mermel, with two brothers. After retirement, Mr. Mermel learned the travel industry and traveled extensively throughout the world.

During the course of Mr. Mermel's life, he has developed a life-long love of learning, is fluent in eight languages, is self-taught in drawing and painting, and loves nature. Bennet experienced what it means to lose freedom and regain it. In the late 90s, he wrote a brief biography, *My Life Story*, ultimately joining forces more than a decade later with Rosalie Cushman to co-author *The Man Confused By God*. The manuscript chronicles his values and vision, heartaches, and triumphs throughout his most unusual life. The book additionally includes conversations between the two authors as they share both similar and differing perspectives on life; its challenges, meaning and contradictions on the ordinary and the divine.